Parenting:
Shaping
the Future

Parenting: Shaping the Future

BEVERLEY COWAN

SKILLS FOR LIFE SERIES
EDITOR:
PHYLLIS MEIKLEJOHN

McClelland and Stewart

McClelland and Stewart Limited
The Canadian Publishers
25 Hollinger Road
Toronto, Ontario
M4B 3G2

Acknowledgements

Pages 9–10, ''Mara and Ringer.'' From Lynne Ann Despelder and Nathalie Prettyman, *A Guidebook for Teaching Family Living*. Copyright © 1980 by Allyn and Bacon, Inc. Reprinted with permission. / Pages 11–12, ''The Family of Children'' by Rees Mason. Reprinted by permission of Grosset & Dunlap from *The Family of Children*, copyright © 1977 by Grosset & Dunlap and The Ridge Press. / Pages 36–37 From *Oh Boy! Babies!* by Alison Cragin Herzig and Jane Lawrence Mali. Copyright © 1980 by Alison Cragin Herzig and Jane Lawrence Mali. By permission of Little, Brown and Company. / Pages 72–73. IALAC concept and excerpt reprinted by permission of the author, Dr. Sidney B. Simon. / Page 104. *The Child as Citizen in Canada*. From the IYC Report ''For Canada's Children'' with permission of the Canadian Council on Children and Youth. This report is available from the council, 333 Chapel St., Ottawa, Ont., K1N 7Z2, for $10.00. /
Illustrative Support
Cartoons, pages 15, 50, 57, 74, 78 from *The Family Circus* by Bil Keane. Reprint Cowles

DESIGN: Brant Cowie/Artplus Ltd.

Printed and bound in Canada

CANADIAN CATALOGUING IN PUBLICATION DATA

Cowan, Beverley.
  Parenting: shaping the future

(Skills for life)
For use in secondary schools.
Includes bibliographical references.
ISBN 0-7710-2304-9

1. Parenting. 2. Children – Management.
I. Title. II. Series.

HQ755.8.C68   1985   649.1
C85-099031-9

Syndicate, Inc. All rights reserved. / Cartoons, pages 22, 28. Reprinted from *David, We're Pregnant!* Copyright © 1975 by Lynn Johnston with permission from Meadowbrook Press. / Cartoons, pages 42, 52, 54, 93. Reprinted from *Do They Ever Grow Up?* Copyright © 1978 by Lynn Johnston with permission of Meadowbrook Press. / Cartoon, page 106. Courtesy Canadian Council on Children and Youth from ''Action for Canada's Children'' Vol 2, No. 2, June/July 1982. / Photographs, pages 7, 39, 41. Courtesy Clifford Cowan. / Photograph, page 35. From *Oh Boy! Babies!* by Alison Cragin Herzig and Jane Lawrence Mali. Copyright © 1980 by Alison Cragin Herzig and Jane Lawrence Mali. By permission of Little, Brown and Company. / Photograph, page 47. Reprinted by permission of the *Toronto Star.* / Photograph, page 51. Reprinted by permission of Birgitte Nielsen. / Photographs, pages 55, 56, 71, 90. Reprinted by permission of Margie Bruun-Meyer. / Photograph, page 82. H. Armstrong Roberts/Miller Services. / Photograph, page 101. By permission of Helena Wehrstein. /

Contents

Introduction

There are many sources for obtaining information about parenting. You can read books and articles; you can watch films and filmstrips, which supply auditory as well as visual information. One great source of information about parenting is people, meaning those people who have regular contact with children — parents, siblings, other relatives, babysitters, teachers, and child care workers. These people can add to your knowledge by describing real life experiences.

Obtaining information is just the beginning. Observing children allows you to test your knowledge and understanding of them. Discussing and writing about personal experiences lets you explore your feelings and your attitudes towards parenting and children. Because parenting involves techniques and practices that must be tested and perfected, skits and role playing help you to test yourself in imaginary child-parent, parent-child situations. Working with children provides you with an opportunity to develop your parenting techniques in real life situations.

Throughout this book you are asked to seek information about parenting in a variety of ways. Here's a summary of the kinds of activities included throughout the book and the symbols that mark them.

- ♀ *Class or group activity*
- ▱ *Practical application activity*
- ☆ *Creative activity*
- ⬭ *Journal entry*
- ⊸ *Research / Observation activity*

CHAPTER 1

Bringing Up Parents

What kind of parent would you be right now?
What do you already know about children?
How do you feel about the parental role?
What skills do you have?

What do you know about parenting?

Before beginning any new course of study, it is valuable for you to find out what you already know about the subject matter, and how you feel about the issues that will be discussed. Parenting is a combination of knowledge, attitudes, and skills. Parents need to know how children develop and what their needs are at each stage. Parents have to define for themselves what is important in life, so that by example they can pass on these values to their children. Parents need the skill of *empathy* – meaning they must be able to feel, understand, and think as children do; they need the skill of dealing with problems as they arise; and they need the skills of communicating love and understanding to their children.

The activities in this chapter will help determine what you already know about children, how you feel about the parental role, and reveal the coping skills you possess.

How Good a Parent Would You Be Right Now?
What Do You Know About Children?

1. **Test your knowledge.**
   Write the letters in your notebook and beside each write a **T** or **F** to indicate whether the statement is true or false.
   a) The head of a newborn infant is about one-eighth the entire body length.
   b) In general, a baby triples its birth mass in the first year.
   c) A newborn baby is not really aware of sound, smell, taste, or touch.
   d) There is little value in reading stories to a child who is too young to understand what you are saying.
   e) You can "spoil" an infant by constantly answering its cries.

2. **Assess your attitudes.**
   Explore your present attitudes about children and families. Complete each of the following statements in your notebook.
   a) Courses in parenting are ...
   b) Most parents to-day are too ...
   c) The best reason for having children is ...

d) The most important value that should be taught to children is …
e) A family with only one parent …
f) Mothers of young children who choose to work full time …
g) The ideal age at which to have children is …

3. **Test your skills.**
Indicate how you would react in each of the following situations.
a) The young baby in your care continues to cry even after being fed and changed.
b) The three-year-old in your care has a temper tantrum.
c) Young siblings want to play together but always end up fighting with one another.
d) A young child seems to have little appetite, plays with food, and cannot be persuaded to try anything new.
e) A young child has been moody and out-of-sorts all day.
f) A four-year-old continually cheats when playing games with other children.

The Parents-in-waiting of Tomorrow

Let's begin by considering the situation for two very unusual "parents-in-waiting".

In a place somewhere far from here, Mara and Ringer awaited the birth of their first baby. Now, because of the place where they lived, things were much different. Of course they knew their child would be a boy with brown hair and brown eyes, have an easy disposition, and an I.Q. of 175 – just what they had requested on their Genetic Selection Cards. And they knew that all the resources – money, food, shelter, education, health care, and things for a good life – would be provided for their child. Most of all, Mara and Ringer knew they would be good parents. The results of all the examinations and tests of their capabilities had been scored by the computer and they received an "excellent" rating. So, while Mara and Ringer waited for their son to arrive, they read about delivery in the Magic Book *(a manual each couple received when they had been accepted for parent status). The* Magic Book *had the answers to every question that parents needed to know about the growing of a child. On the cover were the words:* "Magic Book: *Follow all directions carefully and in eighteen years you will have produced another adult for our place here, one who has the skills and self-confidence to mature as a happy, whole person.*"

In what ways do Mara and Ringer differ from parents you know? Do you think they are typical of parents of the future?

It is now possible to know, before the birth of a baby, what sex it will be. Mara and Ringer were able to pre-select inherited characteristics for their baby – sex, hair color and eye color, body build, temperament, and intellectual capacity. Such *genetic selection* is becoming more possible in our world as parenting is brought about through test-tube babies and sperm banks.

The story of Mara and Ringer listed the resources necessary for the upbringing of a child. Many of these are already provided for us by government and community agencies.

Although many books have been written about child rearing, there is no one *Magic Book* that will guarantee the child becoming a "happy, whole person". And, as yet, there are no examinations prospective parents can or must take to test their capabilities in raising a child.

Suppose *you* were going to write that *Magic Book* for parents. What would it contain? What is important in providing a child with the "skills and self-confidence to mature as a happy, whole person"? You may find it difficult to reach agreement with classmates as to what kind of parenting is best. Parents themselves often have difficulty in deciding. Hopefully, *this* book on parenting will be a kind of *Magic Book* that will provide you with some of the answers.

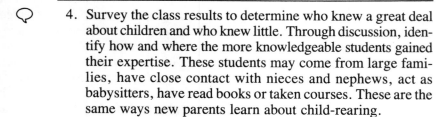

4. Survey the class results to determine who knew a great deal about children and who knew little. Through discussion, identify how and where the more knowledgeable students gained their expertise. These students may come from large families, have close contact with nieces and nephews, act as babysitters, have read books or taken courses. These are the same ways new parents learn about child-rearing.

Importance of Good Parenting

How important is parenting? To what extent are the child's personality and abilities shaped by its *caregivers* - the people responsible for the care and upbringing of the child?

The study of human development and its relationship with parenting is comparatively new. Increasingly, psychologists and sociologists are discovering close links between the care given to a human from conception through the first few years of life and the personality and capability that result. The original caregivers in a child's life - usually the parents - are the *first* and the most important contacts for the child. In some cases, however, another person - a grandparent, *sibling* (brother or sister), teacher, other relative, or a friend - may be especially influential in the child's development. People other than parents are referred to as *significant others*.

In the poem that follows, the author identifies the needs of the child that must be met by the parent or caregiver.

The Family of Children

This unique anticipation: then this birth
This infant grasps my finger
This infant has voice and shape and size and color
This infant has unfathomed style
This infant hungers —I nourish; wails —I console.

This baby speaks my name and walks in my direction
This baby falls asleep on my shoulder and I have never
        kept myself so still
This baby laughs and cries and I follow a maze of
        secrets.

This child holds my hand for safety and assurance
I become the absolute of protection
This child amazes me with unpredicted embraces —
        impulsive, joyous and total
This child puts on my big hat, my big shoes —
    amused and serious — innocently trying to be me.

This young one absorbs my big and little thoughts
This young one scorns and questions

This young one is ready to challenge the past or repeat it,
          to take risks, to know danger
This young one pushes to evade defeat and horror
This young one, casual, volatile, content, bewildered,
          confident, fearful
Ferocious with hope —
This young one needs me, wants me, leaves me,
          loves me.
Who am I to be so cherished and so confounding?
How will I re-supply such love?

     What kind of world do I give this child? What will
this child do with it? Love? Fight? Suffer? Rejoice?
     The Family of Children. The circle. The natural circle
of universality from birth to birth. The circle that encloses
all the meaningful moments of life. The emotions born
in those moments. And the lightnings that play
          against them.
     Look at, feel the morning time of life. This is the
child who grasps tight your hand. This is the child
          who was you.

Rees Mason

What do you think the author is referring to when he talks about
"the circle"? Think about some of the "meaningful moments
of life" and the emotions that accompany these. How could this
be "the child who was you"?

---

5. **Writing a journal**.
   As you learn more about children, you also learn more about
   yourself and what influences your life. How you react to
   events and situations tells even more about what kind of person you have become. Writing a journal or diary of events
   helps you focus on personal experiences and feelings and
   evaluate their importance. A journal suggests a *daily* record

of events. You may not wish to write so often. Each chapter of the book will suggest entries you might include in your journal. A good idea is to record events and situations on the right-hand pages, leaving the left-hand pages to make comments on what you have recorded. Such comments may be made later when you have increased your knowledge and have more insight into the possible significance of what you have recorded.

Begin your journal with a drawing of your family tree to ''set the stage'', and show the people who have had some infuence on your development. Add your written autobiography, which should note special events and occasions, positive and negative influences of parents, siblings, and *significant others*. You may be able to comment on how they have affected you. To focus on such events, you might consider these questions:

As a child, who:
- taught you how to ride a bike?
- taught you your favourite sport?
- helped you with your homework?
- looked after you when you were sick?
- sympathized with you when you were upset?
- gave you your first pet?

You might also consider who:
- teased you as a child?
- embarrassed you when you made a mistake?
- refused to let you take part in an activity?
- made you do something you didn't want to?
- laughed at you when you did something wrong?

Components of Parenting

If parents and significant others play such an important role, what can be done to ensure their input will be beneficial rather than harmful? What constitutes being a successful parent?

It was stated earlier that parenting is a combination of knowledge, attitudes, and skills; but these factors don't just happen – each must be learned, developed, and practised. Whether or not any of us becomes a parent, we can have an influence on children and this influence should be as beneficial as possible. Everyone needs to learn the contents of the *Magic Book*.

---

 6. In the poem, "The Family of Children", the author expresses his feelings about the relationship between child and adult. Think about your own feelings when you see an infant or young child eager to learn and open to the many experiences of life.

Express these feelings in one of these ways:
—write a poem
—draw a picture
—write a story
—make a collage of pictures that express how you feel.
Mount these on a bulletin board under the title: *Significant others in a child's life.*

CHAPTER 2

Parenting Brings Changes

How does parenting affect one's lifestyle?
What is the role of children in families and in society?
Why parent?

Family Circus

"I don't want to see anything that has children in it."

Changing Roles

When two people marry, they each take on a new role – that of husband and wife. Each of these roles involves certain responsibilities – establishing a home, meeting the needs of the partner and developing a good relationship with each other. Each couple adjusts to these roles in their own unique way and, in doing so, establishes a *lifestyle* – their own particular way of living together.

With the arrival of a child, two new roles emerge – that of mother and father. Becoming parents brings new responsibilities. These include meeting the child's *physical* needs for food, warmth, clothing, cleanliness; its *emotional* needs for love, security, trust; its *social* needs of having loving caregivers; its *intellectual* needs for a stimulating environment. Each couple will take on these responsibilities in their own unique way and in doing so, will make changes in their lifestyle. For some, the change may be minimal; for others, it may require a complete change.

Changes in Lifestyle

BAILEY – It's a beautiful boy! Joan and Jack are proud to announce the arrival of Kevin Ryan, 8 lbs. 7 oz. on Dec. 13. Proud grandparents are May and John Bailey, and Jean Riley. Step-siblings Jennifer Black and Jack Bailey Junior are ecstatic!

TWINS!!!
ANSELL – Joel Andrew and Amy Janice arrived on Feb. 14, weighing 5 lbs. 2 oz. and 4 lbs. 6 oz. Happy parents are Joe and Anne (née Davis).

MARTIN – To Cheryl and David, a daughter, Kimberley Ann, on March 18, at Toronto General Hospital. A first wedding anniversary present.

LENCHUK – At last, Margaret and Peter announce the safe arrival of their firstborn – a darling little girl, Stacey Margaret, on April 7 – Mommy's birthday! A special thanks to Drs. Booth and Surgeon and all the nursing staff at North York General, and to all those who prayed for us.

Have you ever read the birth announcements in your local newspaper and wondered what the babies and parents are like? Look them up in today's paper! Sometimes the way the announcement is worded gives some clues as to the parents' personalities and how they feel about this important event in their lives.

The birth of a baby is an exciting time for the whole family, but especially for the new parents. Immediately after the baby's arrival, interested family and friends visit, cards and flowers arrive, father is justly proud, and if the birth took place in a hospital, there is a trained nursing staff to assist in the physical care of the mother and child. When the happy family returns home and is left to cope unassisted, the mood often changes. Especially with a first child, parents may feel unsure, inadequate, and unable to cope with the responsibility involved in caring for an infant.

---

1. One of the ways to find out what it is like to cope with a new baby in the home is to interview parents who have experienced this. You will want to talk to ''first-time'' parents as well as those who already have other children. Try to include parents who have had to cope alone, as well as those with professional or family assistance.

   Make up a list of questions you want to ask the parents, wording them in such a way that it will be easy to record the answers. Be sure to note the parents' background, previous experience with children, and what assistance they had in caring for the baby as this will help you assess their feelings and coping abilities. Consider such questions as:

- Did you have any previous experience in caring for children? If the answer is yes, in what capacity? Did it help?
- Did you take any prenatal or parenting courses? If yes, identify these. Did they help?
- In caring for your infant, what did you enjoy most?
- What did you find most difficult?
- How did you feel the first week you spent at home with the baby?
- Describe assistance you had from family, friends, community agencies.
- How long did it take to settle into a routine?

During the first few weeks, a baby may require feeding every four hours, which could mean interrupted sleep for the parents. Since a baby communicates its needs by crying, there may be frequent periods of crying when mother and father try to figure out the reason. A baby may be fussy or colicky, have allergies or problems digesting the milk, or may develop rashes. In these first few weeks, it is not uncommon for parents to feel there is nothing else in their life but the baby. The responsibility of looking after this infant who only communicates by crying may make them wonder why they wanted this child in the first place.

Once the initial hectic weeks are over, the family generally settles into a routine. As the child begins responding to the world around, the number of happy, pleasurable moments increases. There is no doubt, however, that a child brings changes to a couple's lifestyle.

2. For each of the birth announcements in the text, make up a possible *profile* for each of the parents. This is a description that includes name, age, occupation, education, family background, interests and hobbies, special talents, and personality. Record this and any other information you want to include on a separate card for each person.

Pair the husband and wife cards and make up an imaginary *lifestyle* for them. Include where they live, kind of home, tastes in food and decoration and entertainment, mutual interests, kind and number of friends, favourite vacations, use of leisure time.

You might like to consider these kinds of situations in the husband/wife combinations:

- The couple is very young and have been married less than a year.
- Both husband and wife have well-established careers.
- The family includes step-children from a previous marriage (termed a *restructured* or *blended family*).
- The parents are in poor financial situation or unemployed.
- The new "arrival" is twins or triplets.

For each of the hypothetical couples, discuss the possible effects of parenthood on their individual personalities and on their lifestyle, considering the information you have on them. You may want to mix up the cards and pair them into different couples.

☆ 3. Make use of the special talents of students in your class to depict typical scenes in the lives of some of the couples in the previous activity, through cartoons, poems, short stories or role-playing.

 4. Record in your journal your own profile and a description of your lifestyle. Assume you have just been entrusted with the responsibility of a newborn child. Based on your profile, evaluate how you would cope with this responsibility. What changes in lifestyle would you need to make? Comment on the advantages and disadvantages to you and the child.

The Advantages and Disadvantages of Parenting

In chapter one you read a beautiful poem about the relationship between children and parents and the author's feelings of joy and wonderment in these interactions. A frequently republished column of Ann Landers gives the opposite viewpoint.

When advice columnist Ann Landers asked her readers: "If you had it to do over again, would you have children?" seventy percent of the responders said "No". This negative mail fell roughly into three categories: letters from older parents whose children ignore them; younger people concerned about over-population; parents who find parenthood interferes with their lifestyle.

Commenting on these responses, Dr. Harcharan Sehdev (Director of the Children's Division of the Menninger Foundation in Kansas) said the letters reflect changing trends and opinions of the role of children in families and society. It is a myth that Americans love their children, as evidenced by the history of child labour, child abuse, and the underfunding of Children's Aid programs. Ann Landers noted that one reason for the disillusionment may be that some people enter parenthood with unrealistic expectations and find themselves in financial difficulties, with unexpected expenses.

People who feel negative about a situation are more likely to respond to such a question than those who are satisfied. The article does not indicate the advantages to parenting expressed by the thirty percent who said "Yes".

---

5. Now that you have read the poem "The Family of Children" and the results of Ann Landers' query to parents, list the advantages and disadvantages of parenting. You might choose opposing teams and have a formal debate on the topic. Conclude the debate or discussion by formulating answers to these questions:
   - What do you think is the place of children in our families and in society today?
   - What indications do we have that parents love their children?
   - What would be your expectations of parenthood in the future? Are these realistic?

   Add to your journal entry your own personal feelings and expectations regarding parenthood.

6. Preparation for parenthood involves considering not only the changes in one's lifestyle, but also the demands on financial resources and physical space.

Working in groups, research one of the following topics, and present the results in the form indicated.

a) Use floor plans, furniture cutouts, and pictures to show how an apartment or room in a home could accommodate the furnishing needs of an infant (cradle or bassinet, change table, bath, rocking chair for nursing mother, dresser, diaper pail).

b) In chart form, list the costs involved in pregnancy, childbirth, and infant care for the first year.

c) Plan a bulletin board display that highlights the basic needs of the infant.

d) Make a collage to illustrate the joys of parenting and the stresses of parenting.

e) Compile a dictionary of terms helpful to new parents.

CHAPTER 3

Parents-in-waiting

*What support is available for
expectant parents?
How does the human fetus
develop?
What factors affect this
development?*

In the last chapter, preparation for parenting was investigated in terms of changes in the lifestyle and roles of the parents-to-be. Of even greater importance in considering parenthood is knowledge of the inherited and environmental factors that affect the development of the *fetus* – the human being developing within the mother.

Hereditary Factors

It is still not completely known how much of human development is controlled by heredity. The moment a sperm cell from the male penetrates the wall of the female egg, it releases twenty-three *chromosomes*. At the same time, the inner core of the egg breaks up and releases twenty-three chromosomes. Chromosomes are minute structures that contain chemical units or *genes*, which carry the hereditary characteristics from parent to child.

Some physical characteristics are definitely inherited, and intellectual capacity is also affected although environmental factors have considerable influence on the degree to which we use this capacity. Personality traits such as temperament may be influenced to a lesser degree. More importantly, some diseases and birth defects can be inherited. Within the next generation, parents may be able to control inherited characteristics. For the present, it is important that a couple considering parenthood look into their own medical history for such diseases and birth defects.

1. Write a personal profile of yourself that includes a description of your physical characteristics, talents, special capabilities, temperament, personality, and general health. Under *physical characteristics* include hair color, eye color and skin color, hair texture, body build, face shape, unusual features, size and shape of hands and feet. Consider these same factors in your parents, grandparents, siblings, other family members, and comment on those that have definitely been inherited and those that could have been influenced to some extent by heredity. You might want to note special characteristics of your siblings that have been inherited.

2. Complete this statement in your journal: "If I had a child, I would like him/her to be ... (list physical and personality characteristics) like my ... (indicate family member who has this characteristic).

Influence of Environment

Although heredity affects many of the infant's characteristics, even more influence comes from the environment in which the infant develops and grows. Even in the prenatal period, environmental factors are important. The mother's physical and emotional state, her diet and consumption of drugs and alcohol, smoking habits, and maternal diseases such as syphilis, diabetes, German measles can all affect the development of the growing child.

 3. In small groups, research one of the following topics and present the results in the form indicated.

   a) Use diagrams or pictures to show the development of the human being from embryo to fetus to birth.

   b) Make up a chart showing the hereditary and environmental causes of birth defects and abnormalities. Use headings such as:
   - cause of defect or abnormality
   - possible effect on the child
   - degree to which defect could occur
   - preventive measures.

   c) Determine the dietary needs of the mother during pregnancy, and the optimum mass gain. From this information make up a weekly menu for each stage of pregnancy.

   d) Make up a monthly chart for each of the nine months of pregnancy indicating the mother's routine in terms of exercise, rest, medical and dental check-ups.

 4. Use the information from your research to make up a series of letters from the fetus to the parents (pretending the fetus

can talk). Compose one letter for each of the nine months of pregnancy in which the fetus describes how it is developing and feeling, and what the parents can be doing to help it and each other.

Prenatal Testing

On-going genetic research continues to emphasize in the prenatal period the importance of inherited and environmental factors on the development of the fetus. For this reason, the health and care of the pregnant mother is extremely important.

Early medical check-ups are vital. The introduction of special devices permit early detection, and possible correction of potential defects and health problems in the fetus. One of the commonest is the use of *ultrasound*. As the box-like device is passed over the abdomen of the mother, high frequency sound waves are transmitted electronically to a display screen. A ''picture'' of the fetus shows up as shaded and open areas, which indicates the development taking place, the size and position of the fetus, and the pulsing heartbeat. *Microphotography* permits photographs to be taken of the developing fetus – magnified many times. Where a potential problem exists, or sometimes in the case of an older woman pregnant for the first time, *amniocentesis* may be performed. A very thin needle is inserted into the mother's uterus and a portion of the *amniotic fluid* – the fluid that surrounds and protects the fetus – is withdrawn. Tests can then be made to detect the presence of defective genes or other abnormalities. It is even possible to correct some of these defects by operating on the fetus while it is still in the uterus. Tests on animals have been reported where a fetus has been removed, operated on, and successfully returned to the uterus.

Prenatal Care

Because the developing fetus obtains all its sustenance from the mother, her food and liquid intake during pregnancy should be carefully monitored. It is important that she provides the necessary nutrients to support each stage of fetal development.

Although the mother's diet and physical needs are more obviously important, her emotional state also needs to be considered. There is no doubt that extreme stress and fatigue are detrimental to the fetus. Some researchers today are promoting the beneficial effects of soothing music as part of the prenatal environment.

Not to be overlooked is the health and well-being of the expectant father. His support and encouragement reflect on the emotional climate of the mother. Today's father plays an increasingly supportive and important role in preparation for parenthood and the birth of the baby.

---

5. Invite a group of new mothers to class to outline their personal prenatal care. Include an instructor in prenatal care to outline factors that affect the development of the fetus.

Support for Parents-in-waiting

A generation ago parents-in-waiting relied largely on a network of family and friends for assistance and advice. Today many young couples often live great distances from their immediate families. Young families move more than ever before. Busy young couples may not have had time to foster close friendships. In addition to assistance and advice from family members, professionals, and friends, expectant couples more often make use of community services in preparing for parenthood.

Most communities offer a variety of support systems such as:
- prenatal classes on care of mother and child
- instruction in natural childbirth
- La Leche League (information and advice on breastfeeding)
- prenatal clinics for medical care
- facilities for the unwed mother.

---

6. Contact agencies in your community that offer information and support to expectant parents. Invite representatives to visit your class to speak individually or as a panel.
7. Put together a directory of programs in your community for expectant parents. Include:

- a description of the program
- how one obtains the service
- who is eligible
- the address and phone number for contact
- who provides the program
- costs involved.

Test your knowledge of preparation for parenting.

A. Read the definitions in column I.
In your notebook, write the word that fits from column II.

COLUMN I	COLUMN II
1. an understanding of how someone else feels	significant other
2. chemical unit that carries inherited characteristics	lifestyle
3. person who influences a child's development	prenatal
4. the way people live	empathy
5. period of time before birth	fetus
6. a test to determine birth defects	gene
7. the developing human being	amniocentesis

B. List *five* important factors a couple should discuss before considering parenthood. Explain your choices.

C. List what you consider to be the most important things an expectant mother should do to ensure the best environment for her developing fetus.

CHAPTER 4

This One Is Ours!

*What does a newborn baby
look like?
What capabilities does the
newborn baby possess?
How important are the first
contacts between parent and
child?*

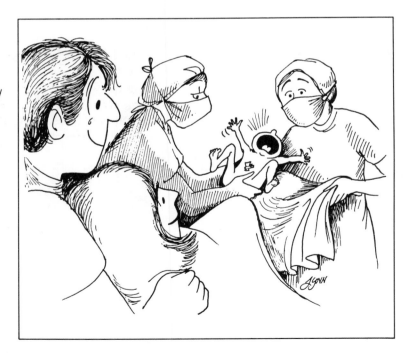

The Birth of the Baby

The illustration shows the moment everyone has been waiting for – the birth of the baby. Today many fathers are present during the birth. A father can assist the mother with breathing exercises while the baby is being born, and they both share the experience.

Why do you think the father has a tear on his cheek? How do you think the mother is feeling? It is quite obvious what the emotions of the baby are! In thinking of the birth process, attention is focussed primarily on the mother, since she does the actual work. The other person for whom the process is equally difficult is the baby. The new environment is so different from what it is used to. From the warmth and darkness of the embryonic sac, it suddenly faces bright lights, a colder temperature, unusual noises, and much handling. A French doctor, Frederick Le Boyer, was so concerned about this that he pioneered a new technique in childbirth. He delivered the baby into a softly lit room and immediately supported it in a tank of warm water to resemble the environment of the amniotic fluid.

Although this seems a logical solution, other doctors have questioned the method. Dim lights may hamper the attendant's ability to see clearly if there are any complications and warm water fosters the growth of bacteria.

Some parents choose to have their baby delivered at home rather than in hospital. This could be a problem if there are complications and the mother and child require special hospital facilities.

1. Select a research team from the class to visit a local hospital and record their observations and impressions of the admitting department, the delivery and labor rooms, the maternity floor, and the nursery facilities. Be sure to make the appropriate arrangements in advance of the visit and have questions prepared to interview hospital personnel and new mothers. Look into prenatal classes, preparation for birth, role of the father, new techniques, and facilities for mothers and babies.

Physical Appearance at Birth

Most parents think their new baby is beautiful!

What does a baby look like at birth? Having grown and developed for nine months in the warm confines of the amniotic sac and now thrust into a strange new environment, how does it cope? At birth, the average baby has a disproportionately large head, which is often misshapen as a result of its passage through the birth canal. The skin may be purplish and wrinkled, and have red blotches. Eyes may be puffy and even appear crossed. The nose is flat and the chin recedes, which allows for easier access to the mother's breast for feeding. Fists and toes are curled and clenched. To the new parents, this infant is the most wonderful being on earth.

2. Ask your parents about your own birth and share information with classmates. Bring to class some of your family's baby photos. Note physical characteristics common to most babies, and those unique to your own family. Use these photos to prepare a bulletin board display that points out inherited characteristics.

3. Plan a school contest in which teachers submit baby pictures to be mounted in a display case, with no names attached. Give students the opportunity to identify the teachers and provide a small prize for the winner. Follow this with the addition of the "clues" to the identity of the babies.

Capabilities at Birth

Although the baby may not be a beauty, it possesses many capabilities to prepare it for the new environment. At birth, the baby can hear, detect odors, and taste. It can distinguish food flavors, preferring those that are slightly sweet, like mother's milk. It can suck, and if you touch the baby's cheek or the corner of the mouth, its head will turn in the direction of the touch. This is called the *rooting reflex* – an automatic response that aids in helping the baby find the mother's nipple. A baby's eyesight is the least developed of its senses. Since eye muscles are uncoordinated, the eyes may go in different directions. A baby has considerable strength, as you might know by the way in which it will grasp your finger. But even with these many capabilities, the human baby is one of the most helpless of all of the world's infants. If abandoned, it would die. There must be someone to care for it and meet its needs.

 4. Mount in your journal one of your baby pictures and describe your physical appearance, length, mass, and any other special features related to you by family members. Include a description of your birth, as told to you by family members. Comment on your personal feelings about the birth of a baby, including your preferences as a future parent concerning: natural childbirth, the role of the father during the birth, place for delivery, and preparations for the birth.

 5. Refer to a previous journal entry in which you described your inherited characteristics. Was temperament included? If not, comment on this aspect of your personality and the possibility of its being an inherited trait.

Infant Bonding

A generation ago, after the birth of a baby, it would be bathed and removed to the hospital nursery, with only a short visit with mother to ensure it had the necessary ten fingers and toes.

The procedure today is to place the baby immediately on the mother's stomach and allow the parents to touch and fondle their child. This encourages *infant bonding* – a strong feeling of trust and security so important in human development. The sooner this bonding occurs, the better. The importance of bonding is evident in research on monkeys and on observations of institutionalized children. Studies of monkeys have shown that, when isolated from birth from other monkeys, such infants exhibit unusual behaviour – rocking, clutching at themselves, self-biting. When put in a cage with another monkey, they are fearful and avoid contact. Behaviour is more normal when isolated monkeys are given substitute, or *surrogate* "mothers" – wire mesh dolls covered with terry cloth, to which they will cling most of the day.

Studies on children in institutions revealed similar findings. Infants raised in institutions where there was little physical interaction with one special adult became listless, showed retarded development, exhibited body rocking, and self-biting.

Developing a Sense of Trust

The psychologist Erik Erikson theorized that a human's personality develops through a series of stages, and is shaped at each stage by the kinds of interactions the person has with other people. A child's inherited temperament can be reinforced – or changed – by the kind of treatment given by its caregivers.

In the first stage of development, the baby develops a sense of trust, or mistrust, according to how caregivers meet its needs. If a baby's cries are attended to, if feeding is a pleasurable experience, if the baby is kept comfortable and clean, if it is rocked and talked to in a loving way, the baby will learn that the world and the people in it can be trusted to meet its needs. Leaving a baby unattended, allowing it to cry for long periods of time, handling it in a cold uncommunicative way, will hardly result in a placid, easy-going, happy baby.

6. Research in more depth:
    a) animal experiments in infant ''bonding''
    b) children in institutions
    c) child ''isolates''
    d) Erikson's theory of personality development.

7. Make a collection of pictures showing interactions between adults and children. Identify the kinds of bonding taking place. Decide how the adults and children might be feeling. Include pictures depicting daily interactions such as feeding, bathing, dressing, and playing with children. Put these into suitably titled collages.

8. Public and school libraries contain many biographies of well known people in which the influence of parents and significant others are clearly identified. A few point out the effect on a child of poor parenting and child abuse. Others

clearly indicate the role of positive parenting in helping the child reach maximum development.

Here is a partial list.

Angelou, Maya. *I Know Why the Caged Bird Sings.*
Breisky, William. *I Think I Can.*
Crawford, Christina. *Mommie Dearest.*
Day, Clarence. *Life with Father.*
Gilbreth, Frank. *Cheaper by the Dozen.*
Keller, Helen. *The Story of My Life.*
Killilea, Marie. *Karen.*
                With Love from Karen.
Richler, Mordecai. *The Apprenticeship of Duddy Kravitz.*
Schreibner, Flora. *Sybil.*

Read one or more of these biographies.

Consider the positive and negative influences on the life of the child in the story by answering the following questions:
a) Who were the close family members and significant others in the child's life?
b) What kind of parenting did the child receive in the early years?
c) What effect did this parenting have on the personality of the child and its feelings of *self esteem*, which is how one feels about oneself?
d) What part in the child's development did other family members play?
e) What was the influence of significant others?

 9. Use your research findings and reading in a class discussion of how parents and significant others can influence the development of a child and establish a sense of trust, or mistrust, in others.

In the poem that follows, a Grade 11 student pretends that a baby can talk and expresses how it might be reacting to the way it is being cared for.

Oh, here at last, I have arrived
No parents could possibly show more pride
Than those who bending over me
Are proclaiming my beauty for all to see.

They count my fingers and my toes,
They laugh proudly at my pert wee nose.
They're sure I'm smiling to see them there,
But actually these gas pains are hard to bear.

Now what's this? The joy has fled.
Mom keeps insisting I'm yellow instead of red
Dad wishes I had stayed a healthy pink
Instead of turning into a jaundiced fink!

Well, well, a new face has joined our group
In starchy white uniform, with a bottle to boot.
My dinner, no doubt especially prepared
With vitamins and calcium and bottled fresh air.

After gulping and gasping my way thru that lunch,
I'm thrown over Ma's shoulder with a definite crunch.
I'm whacked on my back till the burping begins,
Then I'm richly rewarded with dry diaper and pins.

After all that fussin', I'm plumb worn out;
So I let everyone know by a rip-roaring shout.
Guess these folks don't figure I need a rest;
So I just have to shout that I know best.

Oh me, there is still so much to go thru:
Like teething and needles and adjusting the shoes;
There's toilet training, diaper rash, and thumb-
    sucking stage.
Sure hope I can make it to a ripe old age!

---

 10. Add some stanzas to the poem in the text, or make up some
new poems, describing the baby's reactions to various kinds
of treatment from caregivers and significant others.

CHAPTER 5

The First Two Years

What do you know about caring for a baby?
How does a child develop in the first two years?
How important are toys?

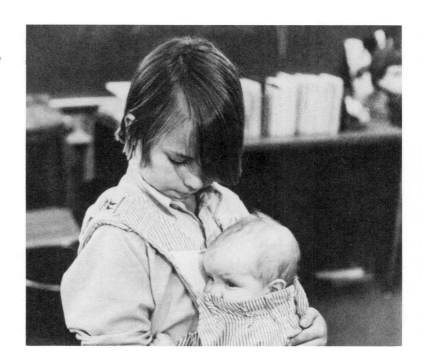

Favourites
and Not-so-favourites

I was a bit nervous at the beginning. I mean, a strange woman gives me her baby and I say, ''Wait a minute! Aren't you going to teach me? I don't know anything yet.'' The baby thinks, maybe, ''Oh, I'm perfectly safe with this boy,'' but I'm the one who's responsible. It's like you're teaching a new human being tricks and developing someone else's skills. It's a challenge. It's fun, but it's a challenge.
—Seth

Diapering's my favourite. It's hard, especially when you're alone and it's a really rough baby. You need one hand to diaper and one hand to put a toy on top of her head.
—Forrest

The hardest thing to do? Feed pears.
—Joey

Being a baby is tough. You get changed when you don't want to be, fed when you don't want to be, given toys you can't do, put to bed when you're not sleepy. You can't run your own life. Everything is done for you. Of course, nothing is done for me. And I have so much home-work I can't go out and play. I can't run my life either. Each of us has our hardships.
—Smith

You know, it's much easier to wash a baby than a dog.
—Luke

My least favourite part, if I absolutely have to choose one, is diapering. It's kind of icky.
—Dylan

If you drop 'em, you're dead.
—Joey

What does a baby see when we're looking at the same thing? What does he think? How does he think? I mean, what does a baby think when he sees water, because he doesn't know the word? We see water, and we say, "There's water." But what does a baby see? What does he say inside his head? He must invent words for things, But what?

−Michael

The only thing that makes you a good babysitter whether you're a girl or a boy is if you can stand them.

−Rick

I've always loved babies. I think they're the smallest, most cutest things you can have.

−Luke

These comments are taken from the book *Oh Boy! Babies!* The book describes a class in infant care given to a group of fifth and sixth grade boys. With the help of mothers and real babies, the boys learned to bathe, dress, feed, diaper, play with, and handle babies.

Which of their comments would you agree with? Do you think parents might express similar feelings?

It is not unusual for "first-time" parents to feel somewhat anxious and inexperienced in the first few days of looking after their tiny baby. Once they have established a routine and begun to master the skills, nervousness disappears and the daily care of the baby can become fun and full of wonderful surprises.

---

1. How much do you know about feeding, diapering, bathing, dressing and handling babies? Think of some of the equipment needed to perform such tasks.

   Crossword puzzles or word search games are fun to do, but even more fun to make up.

Devise your own puzzles, working from lists of words or techniques involved in:
a) feeding a baby
b) clothing a baby
c) furnishing a nursery
d) bathing a baby
e) providing suitable toys.

2. Working singly or in groups, research the following topics and present your findings to the class, making use of pictures, charts, skits, slides, taped interviews, demonstrations with a life-size doll or a real baby. You might like to produce a booklet of the information entitled: *Handbook for New Parents*.
   a) feeding an infant – breast feeding, bottle feeding, schedules, vitamin supplements, feeding problems
   b) clothing an infant – articles, sizes, quantity, fabrics, care
   c) medical check-ups – sight, hearing, body temperature, signs of illness, development
   d) teething – age of appearance, teething problems
   e) sleep patterns, need for exercise
   f) diapering and toilet training – frequency of elimination, appearance of stools, diaper rash, time and technique for toilet training
   g) emotional behaviour – expectations and dealing with problems
   h) bathing the infant – equipment, technique for sponge and tub baths
   i) special problems in infancy – colic, S.I.D.S., abnormalities, illnesses

3. Like the boys in the class on infant care, invite parents and their babies to your class so you can practise and demonstrate what you have learned.

Development in the First Two Years

If you were to go through a collection of family photographs you would likely find many baby pictures. Each new phase of development is exciting for family and friends, and provides a special occasion for the photographer – the first time baby smiles, turns over, crawls, sits up, walks, "mouths" a rubber toy, cuddles a doll, eats from a spoon. Changes occur almost daily as the baby develops physically, socially, and intellectually.

Physical Development
What actually has been happening, physically, during the first two years?

The pictures show changes that have taken place in physical appearance and in *motor ability* – which is the use and development of muscles that permit crawling, standing, walking. Note the changes in facial features, the lengthening and straightening of the body, the fact that body proportions have changed and the head no longer seems so large. Arms and legs are longer and the child is able to sit, crawl, stand, and walk.

Differences in Development

No two children grow and develop at the same rate. You need only look at a group of children of about the same age and it is evident they are all at different stages in physical growth. However, all children go through stages of development in some kind of sequence, and at approximately the same age. Knowing these stages helps us gain a greater understanding of children and their developmental needs.

4. Collect snapshots of yourself and classmates taken during the first two years of life. Note similarities and differences in physical appearance and motor abilities.

   Using reference books for information, chart the stages a child goes through in physical development and motor abilities in the first two years.

   Note the degree to which you and classmates followed this pattern.

Social Development

A picture of a baby is usually taken to record an advance in physical or motor ability. The facial expression and body language often give a clue to the unique personality of the child. If there are other people in the picture, we may learn something of the child's *social development*, meaning how the child relates to others.

In the early years the main social contacts are the caregivers – usually the parents. In the first months of life, a baby is not too aware of the differences in the people who look after its needs. Gradually, as senses become more refined, a baby can distinguish through sight, voice, and smell, the principal caregivers.

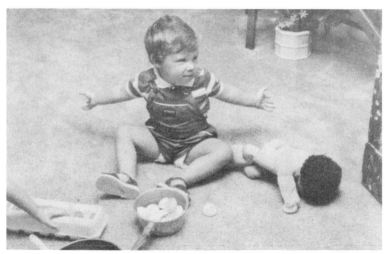

It is common for a baby, at about eight months of age, to display *stranger anxiety*. The baby, who up until now, reacted gleefully to almost anyone who approached, suddenly "makes strange" with unfamiliar people. It simply means the baby can now distinguish between familiar and unfamiliar people. An older child may show *separation anxiety*, becoming upset when the main caregiver – usually the mother – leaves for any period of time. The child knows she has gone and has not yet learned that she will return.

 5. Collect pictures of children under the age of two showing a variety of facial expressions or body language. Make up captions – appropriate titles or remarks – that reflect how the child is feeling or what the child would say, if it could talk.

6. Quiz your own and other parents about humorous or embarrassing experiences they can recall in social interactions

between babies and other people. If you have cared for a baby, you may be able to add some of your own. Share these with classmates including experiences you may have had with "stranger anxiety" or "separation anxiety".

Intellectual Development

It is unlikely that any of us can remember what it was like to be a baby. We can, however, gain some idea by pretending to be a baby again.

Consider what you would see if you sat on the floor of your classroom. There would be a number of very interesting objects within your line of vision.

Pretend you have never seen these objects before and decide what you could find out about them through touching, tasting, smelling, and manipulating them. Everything is an unknown to the baby and as it learns to sit up, crawl, stand, and walk the number of unknowns available for exploration increases. It is through the use of the senses that the "unknowns" become "knowns".

One of the earliest researchers into how children learn was Jean Piaget. He named the first stage of intellectual development the *sensorimotor stage*. His studies revealed that in the infancy stage, a child learns about the environment through its senses. Every object within grasp is mouthed, felt, smelled, listened to, and watched. As motor skills develop, the number of objects within grasp increases; and with the development of smaller wrist and finger muscles, the objects can be manipulated and moved in various ways.

7. Generate a list of all the things a child learns to do in the first two years. Classify these as to physical, social, and intellectual.

When learning about the development of the fetus prior to birth, it was suggested that you write imaginary letters from the fetus to the expectant parents explaining the development taking place.

Using a similar format, write letters to imaginary grandparents from a child describing what is happening in its life and its reactions and feelings about these changes. You might like to illustrate your letters with appropriate pictures, charts, cartoons, descriptions of amusing and heart-warming incidents. If you like to write poetry, use poems instead of letters.

8. Sit on the floor of your classroom. Make a list of all the objects a crawling child could make contact with. What might the child do with each one? What could be learned from them? Would any be dangerous?

Toys for Babies

Providing a toy for a baby is not just a way of keeping it amused and relieving boredom. It is through toys that a child learns about the world around and develops intellectual and motor skills. Toys for a baby usually include soft, cuddly, stuffed animals or dolls that can be pushed and pulled and provide some sense of comfort. Hanging crib toys, rattles, and musical toys stimulate the senses and encourage grasping and manipulation. As the child begins to crawl and walk, ''push-and-pull'' toys are more popular.

9. Collect a variety of toys suitable for a child two years of age and under. If you have difficulty obtaining these, substitute with pictures from magazines and store catalogues. Evaluate each according to:
   - cost
   - safety
   - durability
   - stimulus
   - appropriateness to physical and motor skills
   - aid in intellectual development
   - non-sexist.
   From your evaluation make a list of toys most suitable for the infant to two-year-old.

If you have had occasion recently to visit the toy department of a large store, you will know that toys are big business. There is a toy for every possible mode of play. Toys suitable for a baby soon lose their value as the child outgrows their usefulness. There are many items found in the home that can provide equal stimulation and learning, without the cost. What is important is that a child be given a wide variety of toys or objects that are safe to handle, that stimulate curiosity, and that teach about the world around.

---

10. Store-bought toys are often expensive considering the short time span in which they will be beneficial to a child. There are many items found in the home that can be equally exciting and stimulating.

    Divide into groups to match the number of rooms found in the average home: kitchen, bedroom, den, bathroom, recreation room, dining room, living room.

    In chart form, as indicated, list all the possible play items that could be found in that room. Evaluate each according to the criteria indicated – an example has been given.

Room	Article	Age	Child Learns	Safety
kitchen	pots	18 mos – 2 years	stacking sizes	sharp edges

11. To reinforce what you have learned about babies, take part in an "Eggsperiment".

    Each student is given a fresh egg, which must be regarded as a fragile new baby, and taken care of for a stated number of days. The egg must be cared for twenty-four hours a day, just as a newborn human would be, with pretend feedings and diaper changes at appropriate times. The baby can be left with reliable eggsitters only when necessary.

    Personalize your baby. Paint a face on the egg, add hair, provide a name, clothes, and a cradle. You will record what you do and the baby's progress in a daily log or baby's book. Regard each day as equivalent to four months in the baby's life. Include in the log the baby's name, sex, mass, height, physical appearance, personality. As the days progress, record significant events, amusing situations, the baby's progress, just as a new parent might record these events in a baby book.

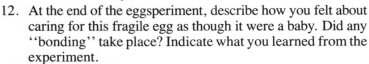

12. At the end of the eggsperiment, describe how you felt about caring for this fragile egg as though it were a baby. Did any ''bonding'' take place? Indicate what you learned from the experiment.

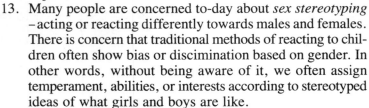

13. Many people are concerned to-day about *sex stereotyping* – acting or reacting differently towards males and females. There is concern that traditional methods of reacting to children often show bias or discimination based on gender. In other words, without being aware of it, we often assign temperament, abilities, or interests according to stereotyped ideas of what girls and boys are like.

    Has any of this happened in your discussions or activities? Did you distinguish infant clothing as being pink for girls and blue for boys? Was there a difference in how you described girl and boy babies – physically, in temperament, in interests, in activities? Did you suggest certain toys as being more appropriate to one sex?

    Go back through your writings and look for evidence of sex stereotyping.

    Count the number of girl and boy babies in the eggsperiments. Discuss the reasons for choosing a particular sex.

    Discuss the possible effect on children of treatment that suggests an inferiority of one sex in relation to the other.

CHAPTER 6

From Terrible Twos to Fascinating Fives

What do you know about pre-schoolers?
How do children develop – physically, socially, and emotionally?

The *Terrible* Twos

The *Trusting* Threes

The *Frustrating* Fours

The *Fascinating* Fives

These are the names of a series of films distributed through the National Film Board in the early 1960s. The adjectives are as much a description of how parents may feel about children at each of these ages as a description of the age itself.

As the titles suggest, all children progress through stages of development. Each child, as we know, develops at his/her own rate. The ages in the titles are approximates or averages. In order to verify if these titles are accurate, we need to consider what is happening to children at each of these ages or stages.

---

1. How much do you know about pre-school age children?
   Think about the personal experiences you have had with children in your family or those you babysit, then complete this statement with as many characteristics as you can. (Two examples have been given.)
   Pre-schoolers...
   • differ in their toilet training progress.
   • can be unpredictable.

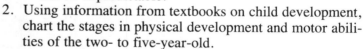

2. Using information from textbooks on child development, chart the stages in physical development and motor abilities of the two- to five-year-old.
   Collect pictures and photos of pre-schoolers to add to the chart in creating a bulletin board display or collage.

The Terrible Twos

Physical development
Compare your pictures of two-year-olds with pictures of babies and one-year-olds. Note the change in general appearance. Growth of arms and legs has resulted in body proportions that are closer to that of an adult. With increased large muscle development, a two-year-old can walk, climb, push, pull and run.

Yet, when you watch a two-year-old walk, you know why, at this age, the child is called a *toddler*. Lack of good body control and balance and frequent tripping and falling is common.

At about two years of age, a child begins to develop small muscles and to improve *hand-eye coordination*; self-dressing and feeding is now possible and large crayons and toys can be manipulated. Still, a two-year-old has difficulty in attempting to grasp and control smaller items. Because of this inability, a two-year-old is often frustrated. Watch a two-year-old try to cut with a small pair of scissors and you will understand the frustration.

A toddler wants to be independent and do things alone, yet is not quite able to handle everything it wants to do. The result is often tears or a temper tantrum.

---

3. Remember your attempts to see the world as a child does when you sat on the floor and viewed the surroundings? Now imagine yourself as an active two-year-old who can climb, push, pull, and grasp objects much more easily.

   Look around your classroom and consider what would now be accessible. What would you want to explore if you were two years old?

   List objects that would provide a safe learning experience and consider what might be learned from these. Make another list of objects or areas that could be dangerous or harmful. Note those that might lead to frustration for the child.

Social and emotional development

Erik Erikson identified the second stage of personality development as a time when a sense of *autonomy* or competence is developed. The child is anxious to be independent and try out new-found skills, but must be taught the limits to such exploration. For the parents, it is the time to *socialize* the child – a time to teach the societal and parental expectations of behaviour.

THE FAMILY CIRCUS   **by Bil Keane**

The cartoon depicts a typical day in the life of a two-year-old. No wonder P.J. is frustrated.

Parents need to be careful that they do not overprotect the child or inhibit attempts at independence to the point where there is a loss of self-confidence. On the other hand, they should not be overly *permissive* – they must not let the child get away with inappropriate behaviour.

The social world of the two-year-old is beginning to expand beyond the immediate family. As language develops, more awareness of the outside world and communication with others begins. There may be exposure to other children, and while a two-year-old seldom plays *with* another child, *onlooker* behaviour – watching and imitating, will occur and the two-year-old will play – alongside – another child. This may be an enjoyable experience for a time, but a two-year-old has, as yet, few social skills. The child's own little world is all a two-year-old understands so there is a tendency for the child to be very self-centred. Fighting over toys is common.

---

4. The cartoon in the text illustrates adult reactions to P.J.'s attempts to satisfy his curiosity. Note the expectations of the people who interact with him.

Understanding P.J.'s desire for autonomy and his curiosity, what would be more appropriate ways of dealing with his actions?

Create your own cartoons to show interactions among adults and pre-schoolers.

The Trusting Threes

Physical Development

Most skills improve with practice. The average three-year-old is beginning to lose baby fat and stands more erect. Rapid growth of arms and legs allow better use of the large muscles and there is improved balance and body control. A three-year-old can likely self-dress and feed with no assistance. With improved small muscle development and hand-eye coordination, there is more skill in controlling and manipulating small objects. A greater variety of activities are possible, which satisfy curiosity and stimulate the mind. Increased intellectual development means a three-year-old has a longer *attention span* – the child can enjoy quieter activities for longer periods of time. With fewer frustrations, the disposition of the three-year-old improves. A child at this stage is usually happy, cheerful, and talkative.

Social and Emotional Development
If you have ever tried reading a story to a three-year-old, you will know how talkative he or she can be. By three, a child is

extremely curious and wants to know about everything. Language development has improved and the child is able to understand simple answers to questions. Improved understanding of language also means the child is more able to understand rules and expected behaviour. The *trusting*, more capable three-year-old is very concerned with pleasing adults and looks for praise and rewards for good behaviour.

Playmates now assume more importance, and there is a marked improvement in the social skills of sharing and co-operation. A three-year-old is more likely to play *with* other children, sharing toys and planning activities together.

---

5. Tape-record conversations with three-year-olds. Try to determine some of the characteristics of a child at this age and stage from the conversations. Share these with the class.

   Share experiences in reading stories to pre-schoolers. What kinds of questions do they ask? What do they learn from these experiences? Make a list of stories they seem to enjoy most and discuss why these would be such favorites.

6. Three-year-olds love to help. Make a checklist of all the jobs a child of three could learn to handle. Transfer these to a daily chart that could be posted for the child's reference, with drawings to depict the chores. Why would posting such a chart appeal to a child of this age? Discuss other methods to motivate and encourage continued participation in such activities.

The Frustrating Fours

Physical Development

Observe and listen to a group of four-year-olds roleplaying and you feel as though you are seeing the real world in miniature. A four-year-old knows everything!

The average four-year-old is very active, has acquired most physical skills, and looks for more independence. Noting the increased abilities of the child, parents are often more demanding and may neglect to praise and commend the child for good behaviour, as they did so lavishly in the early years. The four-year-old, who is still just a child, may react in ways that are "frustrating" to adults – crying, sulking, being defiant, and arguing.

Social and Emotional Development

Where the "terrible" two is meeting frustration in coping *physically* with the surroundings, the "frustrating" four meets frustration in coping socially and emotionally. The four-year-old often attends some form of nursery school or community group, which gives the opportunity of interacting with others in a somewhat structured setting. This also means sharing with other children the attention and time of the adults in charge. At home there could be a new sibling demanding an unequal share

of the parents' time and attention. Although developing physically, socially, and intellectually, the four-year-old is still not able to handle emotions as an adult might expect.

7. In order to understand the possible frustrations of an average four-year-old, role play these "open-ended" situations, acting as you think Jennifer might.

   At nursery school, Jennifer:
   - has been told she must "wait her turn" to use the red paint she wants for her picture.
   - has had her tower of blocks kicked over by another child.
   - is expected to sit still for fifteen minutes while the teacher reads a story Jennifer doesn't understand.
   - is kept indoors because she has a slight cold while the other children play outdoors on the swings and slides.
   - is told by a group of children that she can't play with them.

   At home, where mother has just returned home from hospital with a new baby:
   - grandparents arrive with a toy for the baby and nothing for Jennifer.

- visitors make a big fuss of the baby and hardly notice Jennifer is there.
- father tells Jennifer he is too tired to read her a story because the baby kept him awake all night.
- mother tells Jennifer she will get the finger-painting equipment out for her, after she feeds and baths the baby.

Discuss how you felt role-playing these situations. Consider how each of these situations could be handled to avoid frustrations for child and parents.

The Fascinating Fives

At the end of the pre-school stage is the fascinating five-year-old. By the age of five the child's physical abilities allow participation in a great variety of activities. Intellectual development is such that large amounts of time can be spent on an interesting project. The child is more able to cope with minor difficulties. Less concerned with the amount of attention bestowed on them by adults, the five-year-old may even assist adults in seeing that younger children "obey the rules".

Increased understanding of the world around may have removed many former fears, and the child is much better able to control emotions. This does not mean that the five-year-old is a perfect child. It does mean that parents may be more inclined to find five-year-olds fascinating because parents can now spend more of their time assisting the child with creative, exploratory projects and less time in the role of parental disciplinarian.

---

8. Observe children playing in groups in school or public playgrounds, nursery or day-care centres, recreation centres, church groups, family get-togethers, on T.V. shows. Consider taking slides or movies to record the situations and taping the conversations you hear.

   Make written observations of what you see and hear and compare these with similar observations made by classmates. From such observations, note and record:
   - physical development and capabilities of pre-school age children
   - language development
   - incidents of children playing *alongside* and *with* other children
   - evidences of emotional outbursts
   - problems in interacting with others
   - differences in attention span.

   Make a slide/tape or videotape presentation outlining the general progression in physical, social, and emotional development of children from two to five years.

   OR

   Bring together a collection of pictures and produce a "photo essay" of child development.

9. Observe young children in the presence of adults. This can be done in public areas – shopping centres, parks, recreational areas, public buildings. You could make your observations in the homes of friends.
   a) Note the kinds of expectations adults have of children and how these are made known to them.
   b) List social skills parents expect of children when shopping, visiting other people, in a restaurant, when other adults are present.

c) Note the emotional responses of the children that indicate happiness, anger, jealousy, fear, frustration, uncertainty.

Do any of these approximate the adjectives used in the film titles at the beginning of this chapter?

10. An excellent way to reinforce what you have been learning about pre-schoolers is to observe a child in a variety of situations.

Make a study of *one particular child* and observe his/ her physical, emotional, and social development. The child you observe may be a sibling or other relative, a neighbour, a child playing alone in a nursery, or a child in a community organization. You could observe the child without making contact or plan to play with the child for a period of time.

Record your observations, feelings, conversations. Compile your information under these headings:
- general information – name, sex, age, position in family (oldest, youngest, middle child)
- observed information – appearance, abilities, habits, social responses, attitudes
- interpretation of observations – age and stage of development.

11. During the time you are studying pre-schoolers, record personal interactions you have with children – siblings, neighbours, children for whom you babysit or work with. Note developmental characteristics, if possible.

As you learn more about why children act as they do, on the left side of your journal comment on the situations you have recorded.

Why might the child and/or adult have behaved in this way? In what ways was the situation typical?

What did it show of the relationship between child and child, child and adult? How did you feel about what you did or saw?

You may wish to record and comment on amusing or revealing anecdotes in your own life as a child, that you remember or have been told by others.

CHAPTER 7

The Child's World

How does a child's
environment contribute to
development?
What are the components of
the optimum environment?

The Optimum Environment

Educational researchers at the University of Chicago recently investigated the background of one hundred world famous concert pianists, tennis players, and research mathematicians. They wanted to find out how these exceptionally talented people got where they were. The results showed they all were raised in an environment that provided stimulation at the right time with the right materials by enthusiastic teachers and parents.

Not all parents want their children to be "superstars", but they do want to provide the best environment for their development. There is no doubt that the "best time" to begin such stimulation is in infancy and the early years of childhood.

The Physical Environment

"A healthy mind begins in a healthy body" is a saying you may have heard before. What do you know about the physical needs of the pre-schooler? How does a pre-schooler's food needs differ from that of an infant, teenager, or adult? What are typical food likes and dislikes? How could you introduce a new food? What kind of clothing makes self-dressing easier? What clothing is most comfortable and easiest to care for? What are the sleep needs of a pre-schooler? What would you do if a pre-schooler developed a high fever, choked on a piece of food, or accidently swallowed a caustic solution?

The research and learning activities suggested in this chapter will enable you to identify the physical needs of the developing child and gain experience in meeting these needs.

1. In small groups carry out these learning activities:
   a) Arrange to have parents of pre-schoolers visit your class. Prepare interview questions that would give you information about how they provide for the physical needs of their children.
   b) Research the food needs of pre-schoolers, and survey the food likes/dislikes of a number of children. Based

on your findings, prepare a nutritious meal children would enjoy. Have it evaluated by classmates and/or children using a checklist of the criteria that should be considered.

c) Visit a children's clothing store and report back on the type of clothing available for pre-schoolers, the fabrics most commonly used, average costs, and special features to aid in self-dressing. If possible, bring in articles of clothing or pictures to illustrate your report.

d) Prepare a chart that plots the daily routine for a pre-schooler, indicating types of activities and sleep needs.

e) Compile a list of health problems and accidents most common to pre-schoolers. Indicate, using demonstrations where plausible, methods of dealing with these.

f) Make a list of common indoor and outdoor games children can play to develop large muscles and improve motor abilities and co-ordination. Make up some games of your own and demonstrate these to your classmates.

g) Compile a collection of pictures or plans for homemade indoor and outdoor equipment that encourages physical development. Visit local playgrounds for extra suggestions. Take pictures of children using the equipment. Present your information and pictures to classmates or post on a bulletin board with appropriate title.

The Social Environment

The child's social and emotional development evolves through interactions with others. The social world of the pre-schooler is first the family; later it includes other adults and children in the neighbourhood and in community groups.

Play Patterns

The play patterns of young children evolve in a sequence. The very young child plays alone. This is called *solitary play*. Then there is play alongside, but not with, another child – *parallel play*. Eventually a child begins to play with other children – *mixed play*, and lastly, the child will co-operate with others in planning a play activity – *co-operative play*. This can be seen best in such an activity as "playing house" where the children decide who will play each role and what will be happening.

Such role-playing also follows a sequence. The very young child acts out a simple solitary role. Role-play with two children is more complex. One may play the leader and suggest the activity; the other may go along with this, or decide not to play. As they share in role-playing situations, differing personalities become apparent and develop. Some take naturally to the leadership role; others may be content to take turns and be the followers. As the groups change, the roles may also reverse.

In interacting with others in these ways, the child is learning how to organize and make decisions. Exposure to other adults and children provides the child with opportunities to feel and express a variety of emotions and learn to cope with these in socially acceptable ways.

Role-play can be encouraged by providing the necessary props – play houses, old clothes, building materials, and toys that are smaller versions of equipment used in the adult world.

A more sophisticated and creative version of role-playing involves the use of puppets. Dramatic play allows the child to express emotions, provides an outlet for energy and curiosity, stimulates the mind, is a vehicle for interaction with others, and is a lot of fun.

2. a) Observe groups of children in public playgrounds, nursery schools, or neighbourhood backyards. Record and describe the kinds of play activities you observe, classifying these as solitary, parallel, mixed, and co-operative.

   b) Share with classmates recollections of the kinds of play activities you took part in, and most enjoyed, as a child. Discuss the social and emotional development provided by these activities. Why were they so enjoyable?

   Discuss your present feelings about role-playing. Do teenagers enjoy it as much as children seem to? Are there still some benefits for teenagers in role-playing real-life situations?

The Intellectual Environment

Commercial Toys

A great portion of the child's day is spent playing with toys. It has been said that play is to a child as work is to an adult. Toy manufacturers are very aware of the importance of toys to the intellectual development of the young child. The number and variety of educational toys in the marketplace has increased significantly. You have evaluated toys suitable for an infant. There are many more to evaluate for the pre-schooler.

Commercial toys can be expensive and price is seldom an indication of the toy's value to the child. Often a less expensive toy will hold the child's attention longer and be a more effective learning tool. While safety and durability are still important, the degree to which the pre-schooler will play with the toy is more important.

How valuable is an "educational" toy that a child can "master" in a few days and will then discard? How stimulating is a toy that does everything for the child and allows for little imagination or creativity on the part of the child?

You can soon identify good toys by noting those that children play with most often and for the longest period of time. These are often the same toys children have played with for generations–dolls, trucks, shovels and pails, balls, ropes, and blocks. What has made these so universally popular?

---

3. Using old magazines and store catalogues make a collection of pictures of toys suitable for the pre-school age child. Sort these into the following categories:
   a) building or construction toys
   b) "role-play" toys
   c) games
   d) toys to develop motor skills
   e) "quiet" activity toys – books, records
   f) toys to stimulate creativity.
   Evaluate the collection according to: cost, safety, child development, age suitability, non-sexist role development.

4. From the research and evaluation, make a list of those toys you felt were the best choices for each age in the pre-school years, indicating the reasons for the choice.

5. Choosing the toy you liked best, prepare an ad for a T.V. commercial or toy catalogue that might be used to promote its sale, indicating why it is a good buy. Display the ads on a bulletin board.

The Creative Environment

If you have visited or worked in nursery or day-care centres, you probably noticed that many of the activities provided did not involve commercial toys. Most such schools have *activity centres* where the child can "do his/her own thing" with sinks of water and pails; paint or crayons; musical instruments; paste and paper; wooden blocks. Parents often overlook these kinds of activities as ways in which a child can learn, create, and have fun with a minimum of cost and effort.

Creative Art

Art activities develop a child's concepts of colour, texture, design, and shape, and also contribute to the child's understanding of the world. A young child does not draw and paint things the way they look to an adult, but rather as the child sees and understands things in his/her world at this stage of life. Because of this, we can often gain some clues through a child's art of fears or doubts the child may be having. Creative art not only reflects feelings, but can provide an outlet for expressing emotions and feelings that cannot be verbalized.

The poem that follows tells of how a young boy expresses his feelings in his drawings, and the stifling of this creative outlet as he is forced to adopt an adult's interpretation of how the world looks.

About School

He always wanted to say things.
　But no one understood.
He always wanted to explain things, but no one cared,
So he drew.

Sometimes he would just draw and it wasn't anything.
He wanted to carve it in stone or write it in the sky.
He would lie out on the grass and look up in the sky

and it would be only the sky
and things inside him that needed saying.

And it was after that that he drew the picture,
It was a beautiful picture. He kept it under his pillow
   and would let no one see it.
And he would look at it every night and think about it.
And when it was dark and his eyes were closed
   he could see it still.
And it was all of him and he loved it.

When he started school he brought it with him,
Not to show anyone, but just to have with him
   like a friend.
It was funny about school.
He sat in a square brown room,
   like all the other rooms,
And it was tight and close, and stiff.

He hated to hold the pencil and chalk,
   with his arm stiff
   and his feet flat on the floor, stiff,
   with the teacher watching and watching.

The teacher came and spoke to him.
She told him to wear a tie like all the other boys,
He said he didn't like them
   and she said it didn't matter.
After that he drew. And he drew all yellow
   and it was the way he felt about morning.
   And it was beautiful.

The teacher came and smiled at him.
   "What's this?" she said.
Why don't you draw something like Ken's drawing?
   Isn't it beautiful?"

After that his mother bought him a tie

and he always drew airplanes
and rocket-ships like everyone else.
And he threw the old picture away.
And when he lay all alone looking at the sky,
it was big and blue,
and all of everthing,
but he wasn't anymore.

He was square and brown inside
and his hands were stiff.
And he was like everyone else.
All the things inside him that
needed saying
didn't need it anymore.

It had stopped pushing. It was crushed.
Stiff
Like everything else.
Anonymous

The poem clearly points out the importance of allowing a child to draw things as the child sees and feels them. It can be very revealing to ask a child to explain his/her picture to you!

Music

All children love music – the rhythmic beat, the melody, the accompanying words. We are well aware of the effect of rocking and lullabies on the infant. We have all seen a young child dancing and swaying, with no sense of embarrassment, to the sound of lilting music. Music is the ideal medium for creative expression and intellectual stimulation.

Musical experiences for a child should allow that child to become personally involved in the process or action, rather than a passive listener. A child loves to sing and will quickly memorize even the most nonsensical ditty. Experiences should be provided for the child to make up the words to a song, or make changes in those provided by the lyricist.

Creative movements to accompany a song or melody help the child's physical and intellectual development and add to the enjoyment of music. Inexpensive musical instruments can be purchased or improvised from materials found in the home, which allow the child to beat out the rythmn or produce musical sounds.

6. Canvas your community. Make a list of the pre-school facilities available. Arrange to visit one or more of these where you can observe children taking part in a variety of activities.
   Record and report back to classmates, information about the following:
   a) physical layout of the facility, including the activity centres, toy and equipment storage, kitchen and rest areas, outdoor facilities
   b) for each activity centre – equipment, kinds of activities provided for
   c) how the physical needs of the children are met – toilet routine, snacks, rest periods, safety
   d) circle activities – story time, games, music
   e) outdoor facilities – equipment, size of area, kinds of activities
   f) selection of toys available to the children
   g) provisions for free play and role play
   h) general daily routine
   i) rules and how these are enforced
   j) number of children, age range, number of adults, hours the facility is open, special facilities.

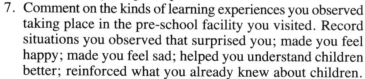

7. Comment on the kinds of learning experiences you observed taking place in the pre-school facility you visited. Record situations you observed that surprised you; made you feel happy; made you feel sad; helped you understand children better; reinforced what you already knew about children.

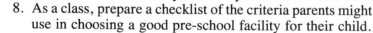

8. As a class, prepare a checklist of the criteria parents might use in choosing a good pre-school facility for their child.

Books and Television

Reading to a child – even before the child is old enough to

understand the words – aids in language and intellectual development. Evidence has shown that a child is able to understand far more than we would expect. The number of children's books has increased dramatically in recent years and selection is difficult. Some children's stories have stood the test of time and delighted children for generations. Others have more recently captured the imagination and hearts of youngsters. Some books are read once and discarded; others are re-read until worn out with use. In many families, a child receives the largest amount of intellectual stimulation from television programs designed for children. Much research has been done on the advantages and disadvantages of such exposure and it is important to develop good criteria for evaluation.

---

9. Invite a group of pre-schoolers to your class to take part in your own "play school". In small groups use your observations at the pre-school facility and appropriate books to plan the following activities.

   a) Describe a suitable activity for a pre-schooler with art forms such as painting, drawing, finger painting, and clay modelling. Detail the initial planning, materials to provide, how to set up the activity, distribution of materials, special precautions. Outline the learning experiences each would provide.

   b) Describe, in a fashion similar to the one above, activities that would involve a woodworking centre, water play, sand play, puppet making, paste and paper.

   c) Look through songbooks and select those songs you think children would enjoy and which lend themselves to actions, accompaniment by simple instruments, and/or clapping. Learn these songs and consider how you would teach them to children.

   d) Examine storybooks and select stories you think the children would enjoy and that lend themselves to actions by the storyteller and the listeners. Consider how you would maintain the interest of the children when reading these.

e) Compile a list of group games children could play and enjoy. Decide how you would initiate such activities, how you would prepare the children for playing the game, and how you would deal with the feelings of "winners" and "losers".

10. Record your experiences and feelings in the "play school" prepared for and run by your class. Note changes in your reactions and feelings between just observing such a facility and actually playing an active role in planning and carrying out activities for pre-schoolers.

11. Research television programs designed for children. Compile a list of the most popular and plan to watch some of them. Evaluate the programs from a list of criteria that could include:
- type of program
- age group designed for
- number of positive learning situations observed
- number of violent or upsetting situations
- kinds of role models portrayed
- number and type of commercials
- ways of expressing emotions
- degree to which viewing child can participate.

Use the results of your collective evaluations and additional readings on the value of television for children to conduct a class debate on the role of television in the learning environment of a child.

The Community Environment

Although a wide variety of activities can be provided at home for the pre-schooler to enrich the environment, many require time and energy to set up and supervise. The added pressure of providing a stimulating environment for the child may be more than some parents can handle. The young parents may live in a community far removed from older supportive family members. In a single-parent family, the sole responsibility for sustaining the home and family rests on one person. Even in a two-parent family, two "bread-winners" may be necessary to keep the family fed, clothed, and sheltered. For many such families, enrollment in some type of community group for pre-schoolers can provide the important activities and social interaction.

What have you learned about babies and pre-schoolers?

A. Read the numbered definitions in column I.
   In your notebook write the word that fits from column II.

COLUMN I
1. special feelings of closeness between parent and child
2. a child playing alongside another child
3. a child planning a play activity with other children
4. a desire to do things for oneself
5. a brother or sister
6. a child becoming upset when a parent leaves
7. a child showing great curiosity

COLUMN II
sibling
sense of initiative
sense of autonomy
parallel play
co-operative play
separation anxiety
bonding

B. Who's who?
   What did each of the following men contribute to child research?
   1. LeBoyer
   2. Harlow
   3. Erikson
   4. Piaget

C. Complete each of these statements with *ten* characteristics you have learned about children.
   Babies ...
   Pre-schoolers ...

CHAPTER 8

Children Learn What They Live

IALAC
*How do you promote a good
self-concept in a child?
Why do children misbehave?
How do you handle
misbehaviour?*

A young child is intensely curious and needs to explore every facet of the environment. Over-protective parents, parents who have unrealistic expectations of the child, parents who criticize or degrade often discourage a child from taking advantage of the experiences available or make the child feel incapable of success. On the other hand, a child brought up in a healthy, stimulating environment among *significant others* who love and respect the child develops a good *self concept* – the feelings one has about oneself and one's capabilities.

Self-concept

IALAC stands for "I am lovable and capable". Imagine that everyone carries an IALAC sign but that the *size* of the sign varies depending on how each individual feels about himself/herself. How people feel about themselves is called their *self-concept*. However, an individual's IALAC sign (or an individual's self-concept) is also affected by how others interact with that individual in daily life. Imagine a piece of an individual's IALAC sign being ripped off everytime someone criticizes, puts the individual down, rejects or ignores, hits, teases. An individual can also put himself/herself down by suggesting to others or thinking it, that he/she is incapable, unworthy, or unlovable. Consider this story of a little boy, wearing such an IALAC sign.

There once was a child who opened his eyes to the morning sunlight. But the sun wasn't very bright in his dismal, shabby room. His mother shouted to him, "Get up!" He started to get dressed and couldn't find his socks. His mother yelled at him for not putting them away in the right place. He went for his turn in the bathroom and his brother slammed the door in his face. He started downstairs for breakfast and there was no room for him at the table. He tried to pour a glass of milk and it spilled on the floor. His father yelled: "Can't you do anything right?" He looked for a quiet corner and waited until his brothers and sisters left for school. "What are you poking around for? Go outside and play," said his mother, irritably. He went outside and found a group of children playing on the street. When he approached them, they shouted: "You can't play with us," and chased him away. He went back home and sat down in front of the T.V. There was no picture. The tube had blown. He looked for his crayons and his colouring book, but someone had broken the crayons and torn his book. And so it continued throughout the day. By the time he crawled into bed that night, little was left of his sign. But since he was a child, and human, when he awoke the next day his sign had grown – but not quite the same size as it was yesterday. He started his day again, His mother yelled! But... it could have been different.

Many things happened to this little boy that contributed to the slow destruction of his IALAC sign. Eventually he might come to believe that he is unloved, unworthy, and incapable of doing things right. Every human being has a need for acceptance. We all need to feel important, worthwhile, and loved. Adults and adolescents have this need met within the family but also among peers, friends, in the school and workplace, and in the community. Where do children have this need met?

For the young child who has no real role in our society, feelings of worth, acceptance, and love come almost entirely from the family and family members. A child needs constant proof of acceptance through attention, demonstrations of love, praise for accomplishments, and encouragement in attempts to cope with the environment.

---

 1. Go over the story of the little boy with the IALAC sign. List all of the things that happened in his day that contributed to the slow destruction of the sign. Continue the story for the remainder of the day, suggesting other incidents that could lower his self-concept. Eventually, the young boy may come to believe he is incapable, unlovable and worthless. If this

---

IALAC concept and excerpt. By permission of Sidney B. Simon. For information about current Values Realization Materials and a schedule of nationwide training workshops, contact Sidney B. Simon, Old Mountain Road, Hadley, MA. 01035, U.S.A.

happened, in what ways might he put *himself* down, as he goes about his day?

Rewrite the story so that the little boy's sign grows, indicating ways of improving his self-concept.

 2. Make up an IALAC sign. Pin it on yourself at the beginning of the day and wear it for a day. Each time something happens to lower your self-concept, tear off a piece. When something happens to improve your self-concept, tape a piece back on. Bring your sign to class the next day and compare and discuss the condition of these signs after one day.

Understanding Misbehaviour

As a child grows up, the expectation is that the child will learn and obey the rules of the society in which he/she lives. This is

called *socialization*. The cartoon shows one parent's attempts to socialize Billy. We are not shown his response.

As a child adjusts to these expectations, a unique coping style emerges. In every society there are well-behaved and well-adjusted children who conform to the rules. There are also children who constantly misbehave. Such children are often misguided, discouraged, or unhappy in their attempts at socialization.

The Attention-seeker

Sally is a new member of the nursery school and because it is her first day, father has agreed to stay with her. During each activity, she runs back to her father for reassurance or to show him the work she has done. When a group of children is asked to play a game she clings to him, refusing to be coaxed into joining the group.

Why do you think Sally is behaving in this way? How do you think the father is feeling? How would you feel if you were in charge of the play group? It is a common reaction for a newcomer to a group to feel, and act, uncertain and shy. But suppose Sally continues to act this way every time she comes to nursery school.

Children act in specific ways for a reason. While they may not know the reason, they do know the consequences or results of their action. It is not hard to identify the reason for Sally's behaviour – she wants attention. *Attention-getting mechanisms* are usually easy to identify, but such actions are particularly annoying to an adult because they are so obvious, especially in a child who constantly looks for attention. But note the consequences of such actions from a child. The adult gives the child the attention she craves!

If the adult becomes sufficiently annoyed, the attention may be in the form of punishment or some other negative sign of annoyance, but the child is still getting attention. Researchers into the problem of child abuse have found that, very often, children will not let anyone know they are being abused because they would rather accept this form of attention than get no attention at all.

When we understand that a child's actions are symptoms of a need for attention, we can meet that need in a positive way. How often do we praise a child for being good? The child's need for acceptance and approval can be satisfied by us ignoring, where possible, attention-getting mechanisms that are unacceptable and giving frequent demonstrations of affection, love, and praise for acceptable behaviour. In the case of Sally, she should be given lots of attention when she leaves father and joins the group, but ignored when she returns to him – no coaxing at this point!

3. a) Survey the class. Based on personal experiences with children or observations of children, have each class member identify a situation in which a child behaved in a particular way to gain attention.

   b) Discuss. Is attention-getting behaviour easy to identify? How do you feel when a child behaves in this way? How do you react? Do you give the child attention? What kind of attention?

   c) List all the things a child does that would be considered acceptable behaviour. Suggest how such behaviour could be rewarded.

   d) For each of the class experiences with a child's attention-getting behaviour, decide how such misbehaviour could be discouraged and replaced by more acceptable ways to gain attention.

   e) Over the next few days, look for occasions to praise and give attention to a child for desirable actions. Note the reactions. In situations where a child uses misbehaviour to gain attention, try ignoring this and make a special effort to praise good behaviour.
   Record this activity in your journal.

The Power-seeker
Joey has been asked to pick up his toys and put them in the toy box. He ignores the request. When asked again, he says he has to go to the bathroom. Mother is getting impatient. When he returns, he puts a few toys away, then starts playing with a puzzle. Mother is getting more angry and the struggle begins in earnest. Joey stomps his foot and says, ''I don't want to!''

"You'll do as I say," replies Mom.
"No, I won't."
"Yes, you will."

Try to empathize. Imagine yourself in Joey's shoes. Imagine yourself as the mother. What will likely be the ending in this power struggle? Remember that as the young child becomes more able to do things alone, there is a desire for greater independence and freedom – the sense of autonomy. At the same time, the child must be taught acceptable behaviour. The result is a testing by the child to see how much he/she can get away with. How do any of us react when someone tries to stop us from doing something we really want to do, or don't want to do? There is the choice of giving in (although we may not feel good about it), continuing the power struggle until the other person gives in, or reaching some compromise. All of us have developed manipulative techniques we use to try to encourage the other person to give in. What were Joey's?

The child who continually gives in becomes a well-behaved, but sometimes passive or timid child. The more courageous child may enter into a power struggle and put up with constant battles. Other choices include: becoming *parent deaf* – no longer listening to the adult; pushing until the child gets his/her own way; or building up a growing resentment against the adults who seem to be so unreasonable.

The best way to handle a power struggle is to refuse to be part of it. Adults generally get nowhere with a vocal battle. A physical battle has a similar result – no winners and possibly two losers. How can parents reconcile a child's growing need for independence with the need to teach acceptable behaviour? For very adventuresome younger children parents might *child proof* the home – putting out of reach the "untouchables" – dangerous, valuable, breakable objects, until the child understands why they must not be touched. As early as physical capability allows, the child should be encouraged to be increasingly independent in self-feeding and self-dressing. The child can be given small tasks to perform, and praising the attempts – however imperfect the results – makes the child feel important and capable.

Family Circus

"I figured out a system for getting along with my mom. She tells me what to do and I do it."

How do you think the child in cartoon is feeling? What could mother do to encourage Joey to put away his toys?

As a child's physical abilities improve, there are many tasks that can be performed in self care and sharing of family tasks. A young child not only enjoys these activities but is being taught to take an active role in sharing family responsibilities. Although the sharing of family responsibilities should be a continuing expectation as the child grows older such expectation should not be accompanied by a tirade of daily demands and reminders.

---

 4. The cartoons in the text depict a mother's attempt to social-ize her young son Billy, and his way of coping. Choose some of her requests and consider other possible reactions by

Billy. Role-play conversations that might take place between mother and son. Discuss how it felt to be each of the characters in these conversations. Predict the possible results of each method of coping, as chosen by the child.

Redo the cartoons, changing the dialogue in the balloons and Billy's remarks to his friend, to show alternate ways of socializing a child.

5. Share with classmates your own personal techniques in trying to get your own way. Are they the ones you also used when you were a child? What is Joey's method in the case study? What else might he have done? Rewrite the case study so that the situation is resolved in a more satisfactory method for adult and child. Role-play both dialogues and discuss how the characters felt in each.

6. a) Survey parents of young children and of your classmates. List the expectations they have of children and adolescents in looking after personal needs and in sharing family responsibilities. List the methods reported for encouraging and motivating the children and adolescents to carry out these activities. Discuss the effectiveness of each.

   b) Recall family expectations of you, as a child, and note some present expectations. Identify factors that encouraged you to take on these responsibilities. Outline some of the expectations you would have of young children if you were a parent.

The Discouraged Child

Jeremy has recently joined a day camp for pre-schoolers. In spite of coaxing, teasing, bribing, or any action on the part of the teenagers in charge, he refuses to take part in any of the activities, and just hangs back and watches.

Like Sally, in our first case study, this could be the way Jeremy gets attention. Suppose the behaviour continues, even when attention is given? It could mean that Jeremy does not want to be put in a position where success or failure might be measured. Some children feel so worthless and incapable they refuse to put themselves into a position where something may be required of them. This may be the result of constant experiences like the little boy in the IALAC story.

Children Learn What They Live

If a child lives with criticism,
He learns to condemn.
If a child lives with hostility,
He learns to fight.
If a child lives with ridicule,
He learns to be shy.
If a child lives with shame,
He learns to feel guilty.
If a child lives with tolerance,
He learns to be patient.
If a child lives with encouragement,
He learns confidence.
If a child lives with praise,
He learns to appreciate.
If a child lives with fairness,
He learns justice.
If a child lives with security,
He learns to have faith.
If a child lives with approval,
He learns to like himself.
If a child lives with acceptance and friendship,
He learns to find love in the world.

Dorothy Nolte

This poem has been widely published. Perhaps you have read it before. It indicates how children react to their environment.

The well-adjusted child does not need to misbehave in order to have needs met. A child needs to be given love and attention for acceptable behaviour; needs to be given opportunities to be "in charge" to feel worthwhile and capable; needs to be encouraged and praised in the search to learn more about the exciting, expanding world. Knowing why a child is misbehaving is the first step in dealing with inappropriate behaviour. Once this is known, we can provide an environment that will allow the child's needs to be met in appropriate ways.

---

 7. If you were the assistant in a nursery school for pre-schoolers, describe how you would handle each of the following situations. Base your decision on why you think the children are behaving in this way.
Child:
a) fights with another child.
b) has to be coaxed to join a group game.
c) has a temper tantrum.
d) has cried continuously since mother left.
e) does everything he/she is told.
f) refuses to share the crayons.
g) knocks over another child's blocks.
h) stays close to you.
i) questions every rule.
j) assists with younger children.
k) wants to be the leader in every activity.
l) cries when "out" in a game of musical chairs.

 8. Make up a list of rules you think should be followed in a nursery school to ensure that all the children will be given attention, feel important, and develop a good self-concept.

 9. Using ideas from the poem, "Children Learn What They Live," make up a bulletin board or collage, illustrating the factors that develop a good self-concept and a poor self-concept in children.
Title it: FEELING TALL. Feeling small.

CHAPTER 9

Supermom and Other Moms

How do parenting styles differ?
Who is the ''Supermom?''
What does she do?

It can be very revealing to watch a child role-play the part of "mommy" or "daddy". Understandably, the child acts according to how the role has been seen in the child's own experiences with parents. Parents tend to adopt a particular style of parenting. This may be similiar to the way they were raised; it may be the result of information obtained from books, friends, parenting courses; it may be a combination of both.

Parenting Styles

To simplify the study, parenting styles are often divided into three main categories – authoritarian, permissive and democratic.

The *authoritarian* parent is characterized as having very strict rules that the child is expected to follow – with no exceptions. The parent is the supreme authority – the child has no say in what the rules will be. Misbehaviour is met most often with physical punishment, the adage "spare the rod and spoil the child" being the basis for such action.

The *permissive* parent allows the child to "do its own thing", providing few guidelines or expectations. Often this parent is overprotective, doing everything for the child, in the belief that this is his/her duty. Misbehaviour may be met with threats or admonitions but these are seldom carried out.

In *democratic* child-rearing the child is regarded more as an equal – deserving of respect and consideration, yet, as a child, needing encouragement and guidance. The goal is self-discipline with the child taking responsibility for his/her own actions.

1. Compile a list of common situations with young children that require disciplinary action. Prepare a questionnaire for parents seeking information on how they would deal with these situations. Include questions on the sources of information used in deciding how to deal with problems. Distribute the questionnaire to parents of various ages. Note the variations between each generation or age group of parents.

   Classify the suggested solutions into the three categories

of parenting styles – authoritarian, permissive, democratic.

Was there any similarity among parents of the same age groups? Did the general method of child-rearing change from one generation to the next? Which method of child-rearing do you feel is most appropriate for children to-day?

2. Share with classmates the parenting style used by your parents in your upbringing.

Recall an incident in your childhood where disciplinary action was needed. Try to remember what they did and how you felt. Illustrate the incident, using stick figures to show the body language. Add "balloons" for the words, but leave these blank.

Now recall an incident where parents were pleased by something you had done. Try to remember what they did and how you felt. Illustrate with stick figures. Leave an empty "balloon" to be filled in later.

Post the drawings on a large bulletin board. Have the class suggest the words that might be inserted in the balloons to match the body language of the stick figures.

Categorize each as: authoritarian, permissive, democratic.

Which category of parenting style was most represented? Which had the least? Discuss possible reasons for this.

3. Noting the body language of the stick figures, the words inserted in the balloons, and the class discussion of personal feelings in incidents requiring parental action, make up a chart outlining the differences among the three parenting styles. Include such characteristics as: body language (posture, facial expressions, mannerisms, body movements): verbal communication (phrases often used, tone of voice); how child might be feeling; how parent might be feeling; effectiveness in solving the problem.

Adopting a Parenting Style

Parents today are more aware than any previous generation of the enormous impact their treatment of a child has on growth and development. Grandparents are often not readily available to act as role models for parents and even if they were the problems facing yesterday's and today's child are vastly different. Parents today depend more often on current literature and parenting courses for information and advice. Do you know who Dr. Spock is? "Parenting" literature began with Dr. Spock. His *Common Sense Book of Baby and Child Care* was first published in 1946, and for years it provided the answers for millions of parents. Today there is much controversy about some of his advice and how it was interpreted. Over the last fifty years, a large number of "experts" on child rearing have emerged and library shelves are full of literature written by these experts.

---

4. Visit a library and local bookstore and look through the section on parenting and child development. Make a list of those people who have influenced child rearing in the last twenty years.

   Working in groups, summarize the basic ideas and techniques proposed by each of these "experts" – including Dr. Spock.

Study of Mothering Styles

In a study of mothering styles, child psychologists at Harvard University's Graduate School of Education made regular visits to twenty-four homes in the Boston area to observe and record the interactions between pre-school age children and their mothers. They wanted to observe the daily routine of such children and determine how the attitudes and habits of the mothers affected the behaviour of the children.

Not long after this study an article appeared in a Canadian magazine entitled "Supermom – Which One Lives in Your House?" In the article mothers were categorized into five types: the Supermother, the Almost Mother, the Smothering Mother, the Overwhelmed Mother, and the Zookeeper Mother. The names almost say what the characteristics of each might be.

The Supermother spent an above average amount of time with her children and there was a mix of mother-initiated and child-initiated interactions. She encouraged the children in everything they did, teaching and instructing them by use of *cause-and-effect* techniques. For example, she would ask, "Why do you think this happened? What would happen if you did this?" She disciplined with reason and often provided alternatives. For example, she might say to the child who was misbehaving at the dinner table: "Either you act as you should at the table, or you will be removed from the table and will eat alone." The Supermother really seemed to enjoy her children, and got good results without seeming to be working very hard with them.

The Almost Mother was like the Supermother, but there were fewer mother-initiated interactions. She spent less time tutoring and did not instruct by cause-and-effect. In reading to the children, she would be more likely to say: "See the ball" rather than "What is he doing with the ball?"

The Smothering Mother tried too hard. She was an overbearing teacher, spending hours with the children in adult-planned activities. Little was child-initiated. The children's needs were met before they had a chance to make them known.

The Overwhelmed Mother had almost no time for her children. She seemed to enjoy the children but tended not to involve them emotionally or reward good behaviour. Attempts at communication beyond what was absolutely necessary were cut short.

The Zookeeper Mother had an *adult oriented* household where everything revolved around the adults in the family. There was a highly organized routine. The children were well cared for physically, but spent much of their time alone.

By its very name, the implication is that the Supermother does the best job of child-rearing.

---

5. Discuss the five mothering styles described in the text. Based on what you have read and experienced through the activi-

ties related to child development, what would be the effect on a child of each of these styles? What style appeals most to you? Why?

Suppose these same researchers went into the homes to study and record the interactions between children and *fathers*. Through class discussion of "fathering" roles experienced and observed by class members, make up names for typical "fathering" styles and describe their characteristics. Evaluate these as you did the mothering styles.

Self-discipline

The goal of democratic child-rearing and the result of the actions of the Supermother is self-discipline. The child is guided toward making appropriate choices and taking responsibility for that choice. Consider a situation where a child must be continually called from play to come for dinner. Instead of the adult nagging, coaxing, or becoming angry, the child is given a choice of suitable alternates and allowed to suffer the consequences of the choice made. For example, the child could be told: "I will call you when dinner is ready. If you don't come, we will start without you and you will have to eat it cold." This allows the child to make a choice and suffer the consequences if the second alternate is chosen.

Many problem situations can be handled in this way. For the method to work successfully, the choices must be reasonable, the adult must present the choices with no annoyance or anger, and most important – be prepared to follow through with the consequence. A choice of "Come to dinner when called or your dinner will be thrown in the garbage", might be hard for the adult to follow through. "Come to dinner when called or you will not be allowed to attend a birthday party next week" is not fair – attending a party has nothing to do with coming to dinner when called. Even a very young child can be given opportunities to make decisions and consider the consequences. This could be simply allowing a choice between two outfits to wear to Grandma's house or two vegetables to have for dinner, or choosing to play indoors or outside. It must be pointed out that each choice involves certain consequences – wearing a newer outfit may restrict where the child can play at Grandma's; a choice of vegetable may require a choice of utensil to eat it with; playing indoors may require playing quietly so that another family member can rest. Having weighed the consequences of each possible choice, the child makes the decison and carries it through.

In the early years a child needs parental assistance with this process and also needs to see that parents and other family members use a similar technique of considering choices and weighing consequences when faced with a problem.

As the child grows older there are increasingly more opportunities to provide choices and give the child experience in making decisions. This also prepares a child for solving more complex problems independently in later years.

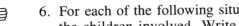

6. For each of the following situations, consider choices for the children involved. Write out the actual dialogue, as expressed by the parent, for each.
   - Child whines and coaxes to be given a cookie before dinner.
   - Siblings fight over the program to be watched on television.
   - Children misbehave in a public restaurant.
   - Children leave toys scattered around the family room.

   Evaluate the dialogue you suggested for the above situations. Are the choices reasonable? Could you follow through on the consequences? Does it suggest mutual respect and consideration? What tone of voice would be used? What body language?

7. In some situations, there is no need for the adult to provide a choice. Children can learn, *through experience*, the consequence of an action.

   To provide examples, complete these ''If ... Then'' statements in your notebook.
   If a child...
   - goes out in the rain without a coat or boots, then...
   - refuses to eat breakfast, then...
   - cheats in a game with friends, then...

- loses a cherished toy, then...
- refuses to take an afternoon nap, then...

Can you add to the list?

How does this technique of allowing a child to suffer the consequences in the above situations fit in with democratic child-rearing and the supermom style?

Which kind of mothering would not permit this kind of learning?

8. In personal interactions with children over the next few weeks, use the technique of permitting choices. Record what you did, the child's actions, and the results.

Comment on your personal feelings about this type of parenting.

CHAPTER 10

Communicating with Children

What are typical childhood fears?
How can you improve communication with a child?
How can you teach a child to cope?

Growing up is not an easy process. A child is often exposed to situations and experiences that are difficult to cope with and difficult to understand.

Childhood Fears

Can you recall situations that upset you when you were a child? How did you react? How did adults help you understand and cope with these fears? There are some feelings, such as fear of the dark or jealousy of a new sibling that have caused concern for generations. Today a child must also deal with those initiated by exposure to *mass media* – television, movies, storybooks, cartoons, and those situations that are the result of family breakups and family problems.

Child Reactions to Fear

A child reacts to fears in a variety of ways. In the early years this can include thumbsucking, using a "security blanket", even wetting the bed. The older child may be moody, cranky, aggressive with younger children, attention-seeking, or refuse to take part in activities.

Parent Reactions to Fear

When a child reacts to fears in the ways suggested, there are a variety of roles parents and other adults play as they attempt to help the child deal with these feelings. You may recognize some of these.

The *Analyzer* attempts to help the child by identifying the cause. In this role the adult goes over every detail, asks many questions, attempts to give reasons, and diagnoses the situation.

The *Sympathizer* deals with the problem by assuring the child that everything will be all right. This adult tends to down-play the situation, is reassuring, and feels sorry for the child.

The *Lecturer* tells the child what to do, stressing appropriate behaviour and how the child should and should not feel and behave.

The *Criticizer* makes the child feel guilty by berating the child's feelings, putting the child down, and expressing what the child has done wrong.

Effective Listening

Have you ever been to a trained counsellor or seen this role portrayed on television? Counsellors do not try to help their clients by criticizing them, lecturing, sympathizing, or offering advice. If they did they might soon be out of business. They are trained to be good listeners and help clients discover the cause of their problem and seek their own solutions.

How do we identify a good listener? To get some understanding about good listening, consider these situations.

Suppose you were to designate two people to the roles of "talker" and "listener". The "talker" would be asked to talk, about anything, for a full minute. The "listener" would not be allowed to give any verbal response during this time period. Would this be an easy task for most people? Whether or not the person talking found it difficult to continue for the full minute would depend a great deal on the "non-verbal" responses of the listener. If the listener showed interest by nodding the head, smiling, or giving any such positive response, the talker would find it easier to continue. Imagine the feeling if the listener looked away, gave no response, or yawned.

Suppose you then asked the listener to repeat what the talker had said. We all know how difficult this could be, especially if the listener was not really interested or was thinking of something else. If it is hard for an adult to really listen to another adult, it is even more difficult to listen to a child. Sometimes what the child is saying does not seem very important. If the child is relating a problem or concern, it is a great temptation for the adult to grow impatient, take over the conversation, and give the child the benefit of his or her wisdom or experience. Consider how *you* feel when you are telling someone about an experience or problem you are having and he or she interrupts you to tell of a similar experience or begins offering advice.

An effective listener, like the trained counsellor, listens without interrupting – except to clarify a point or encourage the talker to continue. The effective listener uses non-verbal encouragement. At the end of the conversation, an effective listener will repeat, in general, what the talker has been saying, to confirm a correct understanding of what has been said.

In the cartoon, the babysitter is demonstrating one of the criteria of effective listening – much to the child's surprise. It takes practice to be an effective listener. Parents and other adults are often too busy to really listen to what a child is saying, yet it is important that a child be allowed to voice a concern and be listened to.

1. a)   Consider the subject matter that young children are exposed to in television programs, books, movies, and

newspapers. Consider the dilemmas and concerns of children of divorced parents, working mothers, families that move frequently, alcoholic or abusive parents, stepfamilies, poor socio-economic environments.

Make a list of childhood fears and anxieties noting those that are a part of "growing up" and those that are a sign of the kind of society in which today's children live.

b) Choosing from the list you have compiled, make up a number of hypothetical cases studies of children experiencing some of these problems. For example, you might consider:

- a child upset by the remarriage of a parent
- a younger child overshadowed by a more talented older sibling
- a child exposed to violent family arguments
- a child afraid to attend nursery school because of the aggressive behaviour of another child.

For each case study, outline the situation causing the problem and a possible reaction on the part of the child.

c) Assume you are family counsellors experienced in helping others resolve their problems.

Divide into groups. Present each group with two or three of the case studies. For each, write an appropriate dialogue between child and counsellor in an attempt to arrive at a solution to the problem.

Role-play and tape record or videotape the dialogue for each case.

Evaluate the dialogues, considering the following:

- amount of time the counsellor talked (time this)
- amount of time the child talked
- "parental role" assumed by the counsellor
- body language of each participant
- solution to the problem
- who came up with the solution
- what the child is learning.

2. a) Try out the communication exercise outlined in the text in which two people play the roles of talker and listener

and each must, in turn, talk for one minute with no verbal response from the partner. Share your feelings as you play each of the roles. What was it like talking for a full minute with no interruptions? How did it feel to have to listen for a full minute? Did you continue listening or did you start to think of something else?

b) Try the talker/listener exercise again with this change. Have the talker sit on a chair while the listener sits on the floor. Is it more or less difficult to maintain interest when you are being "talked down to"? Now reverse roles and feel what it is like to talk to someone towering above you. You are simulating a talking session between adult and child where the adult, being bigger, looks down on the child. Such a position does not aid good communication. When talking to a child, it is much more effective to get down to the child's level.

c) Practise effective listening by simulating dialogues between partners in which one partner describes a problem or situation causing concern and the other feeds back the message as it was received by the listener. Practise stopping the talker for clarification, when necessary, and paying attention to what is being said, until you agree on the message being relayed.

3. Study the cartoon in the text. What kind of a listener is the babysitter? Write an ending to the conversation. Think of other situations in which babysitters might need good communication with their charges. Draw similar cartoons to depict such situations.

Reflective Listening

A technique that can help the adult become a better listener is reflective listening. When a child seems upset or concerned about something, communication can be encouraged by the adult "reflecting" or "mirroring" the child's feelings by saying how he/she thinks the child is feeling. For example, the parent might say: "You seem very angry," or "It looks as though you lost your best friend," or "You're very disappointed about that." Such statements are more likely to encourage a response than the question: "What's the matter?", which could be answered by "Nothing!" In reflecting how the child is feeling, the adult is also forced to empathize, focus on the child, and understand a child's feelings. If such an approach does not open the lines of communication, the child may not be ready to talk about it, or you may need to try again at a later date. Whatever the problem or concern – when the child does manage to express it – the adult must react with respect and understanding not with ridicule or criticism. This can be shown with body language – direct eye contact, accepting what the child says, showing attention by nodding, smiling, touching. Sometimes, all the child really needs is someone to listen and empathize.

Problem-solving

A reflective listening approach and the conversation that follows can often be used as a way of teaching a child how to solve a problem or deal with feelings. For example, when a favourite toy has been broken, consider this dialogue between mother and child.

M. You look as though you just lost your best friend.
C. I just broke the wheels on my big truck and now it won't work. I really wanted to play with it.
M. Is there anything you could do about it?
C. I could wait until Dad gets home and see if he can fix it.
M. What could you do if it can't be fixed?
C. I could ask Dad to buy me another truck, or I can play with my cars.
M. What do you think Dad might say if you asked for a new truck?
C. Probably no, because I didn't take very good care of my old one.
M. What do you think is the best thing to do?
C. See if Dad can fix my truck, and if not, play with my cars instead.
M. Sounds like a good idea. Let me know what happens.

This may seem like a long, drawn-out process for a simple problem that mother could have easily solved for the child. What the child is learning, however, is to find solutions to his or her own problems by using the *decision-making process*.

The steps in this process are:
- define the problem
- list all the possible solutions
- consider the consequences of each solution
- choose what seems the best solution
- follow through with the choice
- evaluate your decision.

In the early years, a child needs assistance with this process. It helps if the child sees that parents and other adults use this same approach in dealing with problems.

---

4. *Reflect* how the child might be feeling in each of these situations:

Child ...
- has just broken a cherished toy
- has been scolded, unfairly, by a favourite uncle
- is being taken to the circus for the first time
- has been left with an unfamiliar babysitter
- has been sent to bed for bad behaviour at the table
- has received a gold star for a painting at nursery school
- has just learned his best friend is quarantined for a week and will not be able to play with him.

Indicate what you would say to the child in each of the above situations to reflect how you think the child is feeling and encourage further communication and explanation.

Continue each of the dialogues to show how you could take the child through the decision-making process, and arrive at a possible solution.

5. Outline some decisions you had to make or problems you had to solve within the last few months. For each, comment on the factors that influenced your actions and the process you used.

If you did not use a format similar to the decision-making process outlined in the text, consider how you might have benefitted from this approach.

Fostering Mutual Respect

The relationship between parent and child needs to be built on mutual love and respect. Reflective listening is a technique that helps the adult understand how the child is feeling in a stressful situation and opens the way to sharing and discussing the problem. It is equally important that a child understand the parent's feelings in situations where the child's actions create a problem and disciplinary action is required.

After being spanked, punished, criticized, or lectured for bad behaviour, it is common for a child to ask: "Do you still love me?" The child sees the adult's disciplinary action as being directed at the child, not at the behaviour. It is important that a child be made to realize that the adult is annoyed at the child's behaviour not at the child.

Child-rearing courses often suggest using a technique called the *I message*. The adult simply tells the child how he or she feels about what the child is doing. For example, if the child has the television playing so loudly that the parent cannot read in the next room, the feelings of the parent are relayed to the child by saying: "When you have the television playing so loudly, I have trouble concentrating on what I am reading." There is no emotion displayed in this technique. The child is told how the action makes the adult feel, and it is assumed the child will consider these feelings and turn the volume down. Most people, even a child, will comply when approached in a reasonable way with a reasonable request. If this does not happen, the child would be allowed to make a choice – either turn down the volume or turn the television off. Approaches of this kind to child-rearing do much to foster mutual love and respect.

6. Over the next few weeks, identify decisions you are required to make or problems that arise. Use the decision-making process to arrive at a solution and record what you did and the result of the ultimate decision or choice.

Comment on the importance of a child learning this approach, early in life.

7. For each of the following situations, describe how *you* would feel as the adult and *why* you would feel this way. Convert this into an *I message* that you could use to explain your feelings to the child.
   a) You discover a child who is visiting your home breaking the leaves off your plants.
   b) A child whose responsibility it is to feed the dog forgets to do this.
   c) You are responsible for cutting the lawn. You find a neighbour's child throwing stones on the grass.
   d) A child has just made a design on your freshly-washed car, with muddy handprints.

8. Interview the parents of young children to determine their familiarity with the techniques you have learned. If these techniques are new to the parents, describe them and discuss their views concerning such communication devices.

9. Look for opportunities to try out these techniques in interactions with others – especially children. Record the situations, the results, and your feelings about the process.

What have you learned about parenting skills?

A. Read the numbered definitions in column I.

   In your notebook, write the word or phrase that fits from column II.

COLUMN I
1. how we feel about ourselves
2. way of explaining how a child's action affects the adult
3. removing dangerous items
4. parent-centred child- rearing style
5. child learns self- discipline
6. not listening to parent
7. learning the rules of society
8. child-centred parenting style
9. expressing how a child is feeling

COLUMN II
reflective listening
permissive child-rearing
I message
parent deaf
self concept
democratic child-rearing
authoritarian child-rearing
socialization
child-proofing

B. Write a paragraph describing the kind of environment you would want to provide for a child in your care.

C. Write a paragraph describing your concept of the ideal parent, giving reasons for the characteristics you choose.

CHAPTER 11

Seven Million Children: ''Kids' Lib''

---

*What is the status of a
Canadian child?
Where do we stand on
children's rights?*

There are over seven million children in Canada – about one-third of our population. They do not have the right to vote. They cannot influence government policy. Their lives are determined by people other than themselves. There are many people and agencies in our society who influence the lives of children, the most important being the family.

Throughout the world, the family is the basic unit of social organization. The family is generally seen as the best environment for the healthy development of a child. Even when this unit is less than perfect, social agencies attempt to keep a child in the family or in a substitute family setting.

Canadian Families

Walking through a toy store at Christmas, strolling through a neighbourhood park on a warm summer afternoon, attending a circus, stopping to watch a local baseball or hockey team, there is a distinct impression that Canadians care deeply about their children. A staggering amount of money is spent annually on children. Communities offer a wide variety of child-centred activities to which parents accompany the child with routine consistency. Yet even children showered with material possessions and given a large share of parental and societal time, can be deprived of the basic human needs of love, security, and self-esteem.

Family life in Canada has changed in the last twenty-five years. The norm had been the *nuclear* family – husband, wife, and children – living separately from other relatives. Today there is an increasing number of single parent families and *blended* or *restructured* families – those that include step-parents and step-siblings. Other family forms that can be found are: dual-career families, childless couples, couples living common-law or co-habiting with a partner, homosexual couples, and families living communally. The nature of family life has changed – shaped by the structure and time frame of the working lives of parents. Work often separates a family and affects the amount of time the family spends doing things together. Shift work or irregular hours prevent many parents from engaging in family activities. Evening hours and weekends are often claimed by work demands, entertaining, and meetings. Work-related travel affects family life. There is a growing absence of women at home as the number of working mothers increases and as more women seek to combine motherhood and a career. In some families fathers spend more time in the home than working mothers.

Most children growing up in Canada are well-loved and well-cared for and are being given every opportunity to develop to their fullest potential. But in Canadian families everywhere, there are also children in need. Children in need of better parents, a better environment, a better society. Children in need include those who have been abandoned, abused (physically, sexually, verbally), neglected, deprived, misguided, or even overprotected.

1. a) Brainstorm to come up with a list of all the people in our society who have an influence on the life of a child. Beside each, identify the needs of a child met by this grouping of people.
   b) In a technological society, a child's needs are often met by agencies other than the family. Use the telephone directory and other resources to compile a list of all the child support systems or agencies in your community.

2. Survey families known to classmates. Without revealing identities, take a count of:
   a) the number representing each of the family forms identified in the text
   b) the number living a distance from other relatives
   c) those whose work separates them from family because of irregular hours, meetings, travel
   d) the number of working mothers.

   Brainstorm for ideas concerning the implications for parents and child as a result of these lifestyles.

Kids' Lib

During the past few decades there have been several nation-wide movements designed to focus public attention on the rights of a minority group or a group deemed to have fewer privileges, socially or legally. "Women's Lib" comes to mind most readily. One of the more recent is "Kids' Lib" – a consideration of the rights of children – children are also a minority group.

In 1975, the Canadian Council on Children and Youth established a task force to look at the needs of Canadian children in a project called *The Child as Citizen in Canada*. On December 21, 1976, the United Nations Assembly established 1979 as International Year of the Child to encourage all countries to review their programs for the promotion of the well-being of children. In its report, the Canadian Commission for the International Year of the Child, revealed these basic problems:

- that poverty and isolation are much more extensive that most Canadians believe
- that adequate and appropriate community support systems do not often exist for children
- that parents need help to be better parents and that this help is not readily available
- that everywhere in Canada existing child-care facilities fall far short of the expanding need for them
- that services for handicapped children are far from sufficient
- that opportunities to take responsibility and to learn the skills of citizenship are rare
- that age-group segregation often creates impenetrable barriers between children and older people and that programs to help people cross them are needed
- that the battle against prejudice and racism with respect to children needs reinforcement
- that the situation of Canada's native children is acute
- that creative approaches are required to break through the sense of alienation felt by so many young people
- that there is a surprising ignorance of the child's need and right to play
- that there is a great need for enriching experiences, a need that reflects the impoverishment of many children's minds and spirits; people are too busy, too pre-occupied, too disinterested to pay attention to them.

"Sorry, sir, but there's a party of four ahead of you."

The message conveyed by the cartoon is obvious: for once, the children are not being made to wait while an adult goes ahead – a situation that no doubt has happened more than once to you. In our society, "kids" are discriminated against in this fashion in many ways.

---

3. a) Assume you are members of a task force assigned to identify the current status of Canadian children. Using statistics over the last thirty years, make a chart or graph showing the trend and present situation in as many of

these areas as you can:
- rate of infant mortality (number of deaths)
- number of premature births
- number of teenage pregnancies
- incidence of birth defects
- number of handicapped children
- degree of family poverty
- extent of malnutrition
- children of working mothers
- children cared for in day-care facilities
- children of divorced parents
- children in restructured or blended families
- children in single parent families
- incidence of child abuse and family violence
- children in foster and adoptive homes
- children requiring special education
- children involved in home accidents and injuries
- number of accidental deaths among children.

b) Using current literature, identify the legal rights of a Canadian child in such areas as: child support, custody, inheritance, education, and protection, and discuss these findings with classmates.

c) Write a paragraph outlining your feelings about what you have discovered about the status of a Canadian child by answering such open-ended statements as:
- I did not realize that...
- I was most surprised to find that...
- I already knew...
- It made me sad to learn...
- I am happy that...
- What we need to do is...

 4. When we think of "rights" movements, the picture that often comes to mind is that of placard-carrying "militants", marching to City Hall to publicize their feelings. Although this may not always bring about the results hoped for, it certainly draws attention to the cause.

Suppose you were part of such a group trying to draw attention to the rights of children. What kinds of messages would you want on the cards? Make up a set of slogans based on what you feel are the greatest needs of Canadian children.

During this course on parenting, you have learned a great deal about children. Along with this knowledge, you have been given the opportunity to develop attitudes and values about how children should be treated and regarded. You have developed and practised some skills in interacting effectively and empathetically with children.

Based on research you have carried out in your community and among families you know, you will have some idea of the extent to which the problems outlined in the Canadian Commission's report relate to your immediate community.

Children in need react in a variety of ways: They become the school dropouts, runaways, drug users, unwed mothers, juvenile delinquents, emotionally disturbed, suicides.

Young families in Canada often live a great distance from other relatives, with only a small circle of friends and the immediate family to rely on. Families are not always able to endure daily stresses alone. There is a great need for networks of support from the community to assist families. Support must also come from governments, friends, and neighbours.

The Rights of Children

On November 20, 1959, the United Nations General Assembly declared: "Mankind owes the child the best it has to give." A resolution was adopted that identifies, in ten basic principles, the Rights of Children.

This is a summary of those principles.
1. The right to affection, love, and understanding.
2. The right to adequate nutrition and medical care.
3. The right to free education.
4. The right to full opportunity for play and recreation.
5. The right to a name and nationality.
6. The right to special care, if handicapped.
7. The right to be among the first to receive relief in times of disaster.
8. The right to learn to be a useful member of society and to develop individual abilities.

9. The right to be brought up in a spirit of peace and universal brotherhood.
10. The right to enjoy these rights, regardless of race, colour, sex, religion, national, or social origin.

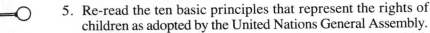

5. Re-read the ten basic principles that represent the rights of children as adopted by the United Nations General Assembly.

   Working in pairs or singly, determine the extent to which these rights are being met in your community. Seek information from agencies and professionals. Report your findings to the class.

6. Based on what you have learned, prepare a position paper representing your class findings concerning current needs for support systems for Canadian children. *Be creative and futuristic in your suggestions.*

HOW WELL WOULD YOU PARENT?

A. In the beginning chapter, you were asked to chart the characteristics of a "happy, whole person", and the kind of parenting that would bring about this development. Return to this chart and note additions, deletions, and other changes you would make now that you know more about parenting.

B. Redo the questionnaires that tested your knowledge, attitudes, and skills. Note what you have learned and how your attitudes have changed.

C. Reread some of your journal entries. One of the earliest described how you would feel if entrusted with the care of an infant or child. What would your feelings be now?

   Make a final addition to your journal describing any changes in your feelings about children, about parenting, and about your capabilities in understanding and interacting with children.

D. Make up a "Magic Book" for parents entitled: *What should I do when...?* Create your own comic strip family and draw cartoons to illustrate the book.

   Distribute copies of the book to resource people who have assisted you with information, class presentations, and answers to survey.
